Winter 2021

CHRISTIANITY**NEXT**

↓

Trauma & Resilience: Neurobiology, Race, Faith

CHRISTIANITYNEXT

An interdisciplinary, scholarly exploration
of Asian North American Christianity

ChristianityNext is a journal of
Innovative Space for Asian American Christianity (ISAAC)

Membership subscriptions, address changes, advertising
and business correspondence should be sent to:
Innovative Space for Asian American Christianity (ISAAC)
4706 Via Colina #780, Los Angeles, CA 90042

Postmaster: Send address changes to:
ChristianityNext (ISAAC)
4706 Via Colina #780, Los Angeles, CA 90042

ISBN: 978-1-716-08922-0

Young Lee Hertig, Editor

Please send submission inquiries to *articles@christianitynext.org*

Cover and interior template by Winnow+Glean, *www.winnowandglean.com*
Cover and interior design by Howard Kim, *@howardcykim*

INNOVATIVE SPACE FOR ASIAN AMERICAN CHRISTIANITY (ISAAC)
4706 Via Colina #780
Los Angeles, CA 90042
http://isaacweb.org/christianitynext

Winter 2021

Trauma & Resilience:
Neurobiology, Race, Faith

Articles

Young Lee Hertig & Jessica ChenFeng

Young Lee Hertig is co-founder and Executive Director of Innovative Space for Asian American Christianity (ISAAC) and a founder of Asian American Women On Leadership (AAWOL). She has been teaching in the Global Studies and Sociology Department at Azusa Pacific University since 2002. She was formerly a Vera B. Blinn Associate Professor of World Christianity at United Theological Seminary in Dayton, Ohio (1998-2002), and an Assistant Professor of Cross Cultural Ministry at Fuller Theological Seminary (1992-1995). She is an ordained Presbyterian clergy and was a Commissioner of the Presbyterian Church USA to the National Council of Churches Faith and Order from 2002-2012.

Jessica L. ChenFeng, PhD, LMFT, is Associate Professor of Medical Education and Associate Director of Physician Vitality at Loma Linda University Health. Her research, writing, and clinical work center around sociocontextual issues such as gender and power, Asian American identity, and Christian spirituality. She serves as a Contextual Identity Formation Advisor with Fuller Theological Seminary's Asian American Center. Jessica identifies as a second-generation Taiwanese American liberative educator and lives in Upland, California, with her husband, their toddler, a miniature Schnauzer, and a second baby on the way. She loves trees, sourdough bread baking, listening to NPR, learning how to sew her own clothes, connecting over coffee, and lightly sweetened jasmine milk tea.

Young Lee Hertig, Editor-in-Chief of *ChristianityNext*
Jessica ChenFeng, Co-Editor-in-Chief of *ChristianityNext*

In 2019, the ChristianityNext working board members decided on the theme of "Trauma and Resilience" for the next issue. Little did we know that this would be an especially relevant topic as our nation has spent the year ravaged and traumatized by the impact of an unnecessarily prolonged pandemic and white supremacy, amongst other social and political upheavals.

Peter Levine is a psychologist who has spent his over 40-year-career studying stress and trauma. His primary contribution is elucidating the connection between trauma and its physiological components. Psychosomatic symptoms are not unfamiliar to Asian Americans and often there are interconnected, underlying trauma histories. In this issue, readers will find themselves resonant with the articles and narratives as they address: trauma from transplants and dislocation, suicide, double minority identity, and anti-Asian American assaults.

Compounded by multiple pandemics, the year 2020 has inflicted trauma from the loss of more than 400,000 lives, jobs, basic needs of foods and shelter, and withering trust in democracy. Although the light at the end of this long and dark tunnel seems to be emerging, the impact of the year 2020 on Americans is enormous. In this context, we address Trauma and Resilience.

PART I: Peer Reviewed Academic Articles

In Chapter 1, *Intergenerational Trauma and Resilience and the Possibilities for the Church*, **Miyoung Yoon Hammer** narrates her own parents' traumas and how they impact her life. Yoon Hammer highlights

Vol. 5, 7-9 (2021).

the role of churches in providing relief for newcomers like her parents from South Korea. A German church in Canada and a Korean immigrant church in Southern California provided her family "predictability and safety" as a community. Weaving family therapy concepts throughout the chapter, readers will be moved to process their own intergenerational familial unprocessed trauma and the residual impacts.

In Chapter 2, *A Church that Embodies a Caring Image of God and Accompanies the Lives of Families that are Suicide-Bereaved*, **Eser Kim** addresses the alarming rate of suicide among Asian Americans aged 15 to 24 (2017). The psychological shock among the surviving families of adolescences who have died by suicide is exacerbated by the lack of resources and support. Kim is calling the body of Christ to break the silence and offer support for the traumatized and silenced family members.

In Chapter 3, *God's Shalom to All of Ourselves: Integrating the Asian American Double Self*, **Daniel Lee** uses the lens of trauma studies to understand Asian American identity as fragmented, lacking integration. Lee envisions the journey toward an integrated self as a healing process from racial traumas, which is reflected as seeking God's shalom to all of our disparate parts.

PART II: Narrative Articles

In Chapter 4, *Trauma & Resilience of the Burma Diaspora Christians*, **Florence Li** depicts the survival of a refugee mother in Hong Kong who fled the Communist takeover in the 1950s. Li connects her own family refugee history with the Burmese diaspora refugees' pilgrimage. Her calling into the American Baptist Home Mission Societies (ABHMS), as the National Coordinator for Asian Ministries, has given her the opportunity to serve twenty-eight Asian language groups. Throughout the chapter, the stories of trauma and resilience fill the pages.

In Chapter 5, *Thawing Frozen Traumas: A Daughter's Journey Home*, **Anna Kang** traces her trauma from her family of origin in Korea. At a young and vulnerable age, she went through loss and multiple abandonments. Kang's longing for a loving mother, and desire for belongingness, takes her on a path where she initially felt nurtured, but ended up in an unimaginable condition. Her resilience of facing, rather than covering up, layers of trauma is inspiring and honorable.

Articles

Miyoung Yoon Hammer

Miyoung Yoon Hammer, PhD, LMFT, is a professor of Marriage and Family Therapy at Fuller Theological Seminary. Her clinical specialization is in Medical Family Therapy and Restoration Therapy and her commitment as a professor and clinical supervisor is in developing cultural and racial consciousness in the self-of-the-therapist process. Dr. Yoon Hammer lives in Pasadena, CA with her husband and three children.

Intergenerational Trauma and Resilience and the Possibilities for the Church

Miyoung Yoon Hammer
Fuller Theological Seminary

Abstract: This article explores intergenerational trauma and resiliency in Asian American families and communities and the ways the Christian church can serve as a resource to individuals and families affected by trauma. The study of trauma is prevalent in academic and clinical research and has gained traction as a legitimate mental health consideration among the general public. However, there is more to be understood about the effects of trauma across generations and within cultural groups. Psychological and social idioms of distress vary by culture and are often shaped by circumstances. Thus, it is important to contextualize intergenerational trauma and to concomitantly understand resiliency within the sociocultural context. Historical narratives of Asian American migration and current experiences related to the health and social pandemics are referenced.

Keywords: intergenerational trauma, resiliency, Asian American, migration, Resiliency Model of Family Stress

We have begun to understand how overwhelming experiences affect our innermost sensations and our relationship to our physical reality—the core of who we are. We have learned that trauma is not just an event that took place sometime in the past it is also the imprint left by that experience on mind, brain, and body.

-Van Der Kolk (2014), The Body Keeps the Score

As a second-generation Korean American, born of parents who

Vol. 5, 13-28 (2021).

immigrated to North America (Canada to be exact) in the 1960s, I am often struck by the fact that the generation of Asian and Asian American parents, grandparents, and even my contemporaries who endured events such as the Korean War, the Vietnam War, Japanese internment in the U.S., and the Khmer Rouge (just to name a few), are living reminders of the trauma, loss, and survival of those events. There are countless conflicts, wars, and natural disasters that have occurred over time and throughout the world, recapitulating historical tragedies and reminding us of our fragile humanity. However, the generation of my parents and grandparents who are still alive to tell their stories of survival, often do not talk about their experiences. They survived wars, conflicts, and tragedies during the mid-1900s, but instead of telling their narratives of loss and survival through oral history or written accounts, they quietly and implicitly tell it through the life they build in America. Although this is not the case for all survivors of these generations, it is a common response. In some instances where there has been mass, communal trauma, the conspiracy of silence, an implicit rule to remain silent about the trauma, serves as a protective response to the trauma, causing unintended secondary pain and difficulty for those who remain in the dens of silence.[1]

I long for my parents to talk about their losses yielded by war and displacement, and to express their emotions. Based on my Western perspective of emotional and psychological health, I am partial to problem-focused coping whereby the emotional and psychological burdens they carry in the deep recesses of their memories are released. But this is not in their coping repertoire and I have come to accept that we have different approaches to coping. Nevertheless, I experienced the way their traumatic losses impacted our family and know that some of the pain that I continue to carry in my own life is connected to those losses. This intergenerational trauma—the transmission of the impact of those traumatic experiences to my brother and me through their actions, inactions, and expressed values—has played out in distinct ways. As an adult, I have come to understand that my experiences of growing up in an immigrant family, particularly with a father who lost his family, his home, and his country, were very much marked by that trauma.

At the same time, there was dissonance between the two parts of

---

[1] Ia Xiong, "Interrupting the Conspiracy of Silence: Historical Trauma and the Experiences of Hmong American Women," in *Dissertation Abstracts International: Section B: The Sciences and Engineering* (2016), 77:6B(E).

our family narrative: on the one hand a life defined by war and loss that my parents lived in Korea, and a life of stability and deep-rooted security that my parents built for our family in Southern California. The dissonance is understandable, considering my lack of proximal relationship to time and space which removes me from those events that occurred on distant shores, and the reality, as well as the consequences of such events, tend to be elusive. Furthermore, I have no points of reference from personal experience that would parallel my parents' experiences of war. Despite a few stories I have heard about the war, the Korea I visited during my childhood and adulthood years had no obvious remnants of the war. The country had become Westernized in the 70s and 80s and underwent dramatic cultural and social changes. But perhaps the most compelling factor that contributed to the disconnect between these two aspects of my family narrative resulted from the fact that my parents and their peers in my community, rarely talked about their experiences.

Members of the Korean American community in which I grew up, tended to deal with tragedy by quietly suffering through historical traumas on personal, familial, and communal levels. This tendency is not generalizable to all Asian Americans and is not meant to disregard those who have valiantly lifted their voices in protest against wars, regimes, oppressive forces, discrimination, and have decried systems of injustice. In fact, while some Asian Americans have suffered silently amidst oppressive social forces in the majority culture, there have been many who have fought, advocated, mobilized, and protested for justice, basic rights, and restored dignity among Asian Americans.[2] And yet, in the cases where silence is pervasive, there is greater likelihood of gaps in our knowledge about our own histories. For example, I recently learned about the wave of migration that occurred from East Asia to the Americas during the mid-1800s. This particular wave was driven mostly by the pursuit of labor in the Western world, particularly North and South America. My father, Won Yoon, is a sociologist who has devoted much of his research, writing, and teaching to the subject of East Asian migration over a hundred-year period, starting from the late 1700s and early 1800s. He describes these migration stories as "tragic," where the narrative arc for Asian laborers was commonly one that began with hopes for economic gain through la-

---

[2] Nita Tewari & Alvin N. Alvarez, *Asian American Psychology: Current Perspectives*, (New York, NY: Taylor & Francis Group, 2009).

bor in the West and ended with the loss of life and dignity. Asian laborers experienced hardship, and sometimes death, on the transport ships to the new world, enduring deplorable living conditions, finding themselves in socially and physically degrading circumstances, living in squalor conditions, and oftentimes in countries different from where they were told they would settle. If the Asian laborers survived the journey, they experienced discrimination, abuse, exploitation, and dehumanization in the new country.[3] My father's desire in researching and writing about this aspect of the East Asian diaspora in the West is to illuminate these stories and allow for a much fuller historical narrative of Asian migration to emerge, perhaps in ways he does not illuminate his own story.

When I first learned about this early wave of migration, I was disturbed by the stories and further dismayed by my limited awareness of this chapter of Asian American migration history. These accounts have been told and recorded by some, but generally remain out of view. This gap in our narrative as Asian Americans further contributes to the disconnect between the historical traumas of our Asian American ancestors and our current realities, even though the consequences of those traumatic events persist in the lives of subsequent generations who live in entirely different times and places. History is prologue, making my ancestors' and my parents' narratives the starting points of my own narrative. I believe that my own parents' stories of surviving the Korean War are very much my story and, although I did not live through those experiences firsthand, I have both benefited and suffered from the consequences of their experiences by way of the impact of intergenerational trauma.

Multigenerational Transmission Processes & Intergenerational Trauma

In the field of family therapy, there is a concept called the "multigenerational transmission process." This term refers to the transmission of relational dynamics, attitudes, values, and behaviors from one generation to the next. Bowenian family therapists focus mostly on emotional-relational interaction patterns, but the concept of multigenerational transmission can also be more broadly applied to family legacies, rules,

---

[3] Won K. Yoon, *Asian Tragedies in the Americas: Chinese, Japanese, and Korean Stories*, (Washington, D.C.: Lexington Books, forthcoming).

and behaviors that transcend generations, either consciously or unconsciously. These attitudes, behaviors, and interaction patterns are passed down through a variety of ways, including learned behavior and cultural practices that are embedded within formal customs or everyday routines. These patterns and processes, also referred to as family legacies and family rules, can be positive, highlighting strengths of a family system such as relational cohesion, stable SES, intact marriages, or value in education. Alternatively, patterns such as relationship cutoffs, substance abuse, and addiction, can be negative, demonstrating ways that the family system is challenged or constrained. Marriage and family therapists employ ecosystemic and developmental frameworks when conceptualizing matters of identity, interaction patterns, and relational contexts within individual, families, and communities over time. These frameworks help situate individuals and families within broader social contexts in an effort to understand patterns and processes that transcend generations.

As these examples demonstrate, legacies vary in scope and variety. Whereas some family legacies perpetuate dysfunctional relational patterns and behavioral cycles that are seemingly impenetrable, other legacies might be emblematic of a family's internal resources such as hardiness and cohesion, or their external resources such as social support and community identification. In some instances, there may be a family legacy that concurrently challenges and strengthens the family, such as a genetic health condition that creates a certain vulnerability for which the family has developed a resilient coping response that has been passed down across generations. Thus, we understand that family processes, relational patterns, and beliefs can be passed from one generation to the next through patterns of interaction, oral history, customs and rituals, and learned behaviors. Whether it is biological DNA or cultural DNA, what is passed from one generation to the next is done with varying degrees of intention and awareness.

As we better understand multigenerational transmission processes within a family system, it is important to wonder about how these processes might be expressions of cultural norms or how they may they have been mediated by traumatic experiences related to loss, migration, or discrimination. How do factors within the family's ecological context facilitate or complicate the family's acculturation process or their access to social resources? Celia Falicov developed the multidimensional comparative framework as a tool to situate families at the intersection of migration narrative, ecological context, family organization, and family developmental life cycle stage.[4] Each dimension delineates important information about the family, but together all four dimensions tell a much fuller story about the family's resources and challenges, resiliencies, and vulnerabilities.

For example, consider a family that is traditionally patriarchal based on the Confucian value of prescribed hierarchical relational structures that prioritize male members of the system to maintain social harmony. When the family is embedded in a social context that affirms this organizational structure, there is relational congruence and diminished likelihood for dissonance within the system. However, when that same family migrates and re-settles into a social context where the majority culture places value on individuality and prioritizes entitlements related to gender equity and personal agency, this new socio-cultural context can be disruptive to the individual and family system, upending the system of patriarchy in certain aspects of life. Please note that the point of this example is not to deliberate whether Confucian-based patriarchy is right or wrong, but rather to punctuate the importance of understanding whether the family's values align congruently with the community and society in which they live. Particularly for immigrant families, the dissonance stemming from cultural differences in fundamental worldviews and practices is what causes much of what we refer to as acculturative stress.

There is a degree of acculturative stress that is appropriate and expected for all immigrants. However, the likelihood that acculturative stress will become chronic and lead to deleterious effects on both the individuals and the larger family system depends on the family's available resources, its ability to be flexibly adaptive, and the well-being of individual members and the family system. Furthermore, factors such as language, the reason for migration, their interaction with the majority culture, their ability to preserve traditional values, the individual's and family's developmental stage, the degree of volition regarding migration, and the ecological context of the family's new community, contribute to psychological, physical, and relational well-being. The interplay between culture, context, individual disposition, and family dynamics is important to consider when understanding the effects of trauma over generations. It is important to note that while family processes provide insight about individual and

---

[4] Celia J. Falicov, "Training to Think Culturally: A Multidimensional Comparative Framework," *Family Process* 34, (1995): 373-388.

family outcomes, and have been fundamental to the family systems perspective, the role that culture, both majority and minority, play in those very same processes has not always been accounted for.

Intergenerational trauma occurs through the multigenerational transmission process, whereby the effects of trauma that is experienced by one generation can have an impact on subsequent generations through patterned behaviors and beliefs of pathology as well as resiliency, which must be considered within the context of the broader ecological context in which the family exists.[5] The behaviors and beliefs that were generated in the context of trauma transcend generations and often outlast the meaning that underlies them. I can trace my own anxieties, related to place and relational belonging to the ongoing theme in my family growing up, about being rooted in one place and the value of belonging to the broader Korean community through particular types of relationships. I recognize that part of my present wrestling with this notion of belonging is attributed to my experience as a bicultural person. But I can also see the handprints of my father's story, as a child refugee, orphaned and living on the streets of a war-torn country, on that particular struggle with belonging in my own life. My parents demonstrated a resilient response to their own loss by rooting our family deeply into our community and instilling in us the value of relational fidelity and belonging. My experience growing up in a stable home and community was a gift and undoubtedly a benefit to my social and psychological well-being. At the same time, there was an ongoing familial struggle with the fact that among our extended family, we were the only family in the U.S. Although the Korean church served as our proxy extended family, there were consistent reminders that we were alone as a family and as my parents expressed their desire for family connection and deeper belonging to the Korean community, this created in me a degree of angst that I can still recall at times. There was a coexisting struggle and a resilience that was a by-product of the complicated and deep-seated effects of trauma in my parents that I internalized.

We are learning more everyday about how the transmission of trauma from one generation to the next has impact on psychological and social functioning, as well as physical health. A joint research study,

---

[5] Yael Danieli, et al., "Multigenerational Legacies of Trauma: Modeling the What and How of Transmission," *American Journal of Orthopsychiatry* 86, no. 6, (2016): 639-651, doi: 10.1037/ort0000145.
Nathan P.F. Kellermann, "Psychopathology in Children of Holocaust Survivors: A Review of the Research Literature," *Israel Journal of Psychiatry and Related Sciences* 38, no. 1 (2001): 36–46.

conducted by Kaiser Permanente and the Center for Disease Control in the late 1990s, led to the findings that adverse experiences in early childhood—such as abuse, parental divorce, and death of a loved one—can lead to levels of toxic stress that increase the risk factors for acute and chronic social and health conditions in adulthood, such as certain types of cancer, obesity, pulmonary disease, alcoholism, heart disease, stroke, and other life-threatening conditions.[6] These adverse childhood experiences (ACEs) also increase risk for depression, anxiety, and other mental health pathology that can have significant impact on whether a parent is emotionally or physically available to provide a secure environment and care for their children. This is a way that parental trauma has direct impact on children, placing them at risk for their own ACEs and setting in motion a cycle of intergenerational trauma.[7] Furthermore, the field of epigenetics reveal the ways that the transmission of trauma may occur through multi-faceted pathways, including the cellular molecular level of our DNA.[8] The studies began with mice where the behavior of maternal withdrawal had impact on parenting behaviors such as licking and tending to the offspring mice. Those offspring mice yielded lower scores of health and clinically demonstrated lower rates of growth and thriving. Human studies have shown similar results and like the ACEs study, reinforce the fact that trauma is not an individual phenomenon, but rather has systemic and intergenerational implications.

Resiliency

The constructs of trauma and resiliency go hand in hand because in the context of trauma, our inherently human drive to survive is aroused. Just as trauma can be intergenerationally transmitted, so is the case with resiliency. Resilience is generally defined as the ability to adapt in the face

---

[6] V. J. Felitti, et al., "Relationship of Childhood Abuse and Household Dysfunction to Many of the Leading Causes of Death in Adults: The Adverse Childhood Experiences (ACE) Study," *American Journal of Preventive Medicine* 56, no. 6 (2019): 774–786, https://doi-org.fuller.idm.oclc.org/10.1016/j.amepre.2019.04.001.

[7] K. W. Choi, "Postpartum Depression in the Intergenerational Transmission of Child Maltreatment: Longitudinal Dvidence from Global Settings," in *Dissertation Abstracts International: Section B: The Sciences and Engineering* (2018), 78:12–B(E).

[8] T. Y. Kim, et al., "Epigenetic Alterations of the BDNF Gene in Combat-Related Post-Traumatic Stress Disorder," *Acta Psychiatrica Scandinavica* 135, no. 2 (2017): 170–179, https://doi org.fuller.idm.oclc.org/10.1111/acps.12675.
B. M. Lester, et al., "Epigenetic Basis for the Development of Depression in Children," *Clinical Obstetrics and Gynecology* 56, no. 3 (2013): 556–565, https://doi.org/10.1097/GRF.0b013e318299d2a8.

of adversity, trauma, stressful situations, and to, in some cases, experience growth from those experiences, also known as posttraumatic growth.[9] We know that two people can encounter the same stressful event and have opposite responses—one person adapts while the other person gets stuck. What makes the difference between these two people? This question suggests that resilience may be a person's ability to experience post-traumatic growth as a result of possessing a pre-disposed, fixed trait, meaning that some people are resilient while others are not. However, in their exploration of resiliency among clients who have experienced significant psychopathology, Waugh and Koster (2015) suggest that resiliency is a dynamic process rather than a fixed trait and can be conceptualized as a trajectory, rather than a characteristic. Thus, as we consider that same question about two people experiencing the same stressful event, one person might be able to quickly adapt to the situation and find a path forward to recovery, while the second person may be initially paralyzed by the stress but has the potential to gradually acquire the internal and/or external resources to get unstuck and move towards recovery. Resiliency has historically been conceptualized as an individual matter and the primary locus of change is the individual client. But this latter process of resiliency that relies on one's potential, and the utilization of resources, is expansive and accounts for cultural and communal factors that contribute to individual, family, and community resiliency.

In the early 1990s, family science researchers McCubbin and Thompson moved forward the Resiliency Model of Family Stress, Adjustment and Adaptation (see Figure 1) (1991) which continues to provide the conceptual foundation for theories and frameworks in the field of family therapy. In their work, they identified key factors that determine whether a family confronted with a stressful event (A) will move toward adaptation or crisis (X). The key factors included: existing vulnerabilities (V), family typology (T), how they make meaning of the event (C), their resistance resources (B) such as social support, and their capacity for problem-solving (PSC).

---

[9] Marcela C. Weber, et al., "Modeling Resilience, Meaning in Life, Posttraumatic Growth, and Disaster Preparedness with Two Samples of Tornado Survivors," *Traumatology* 26, no. 3 (2020): 266-277, http://dx.doi.org/10.1037/trm0000210.

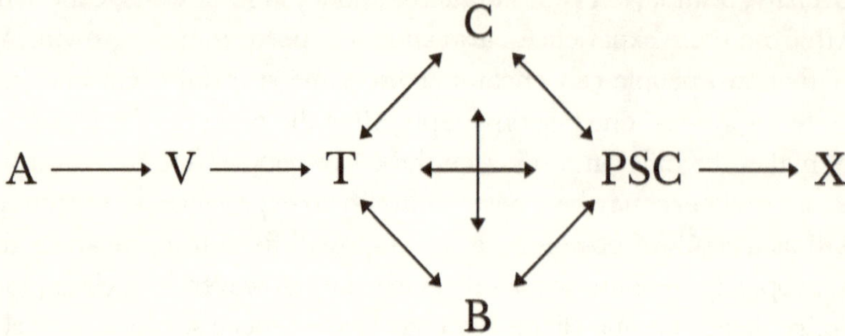

Figure 1

This model is helpful in understanding family response to stress at a micro level as well as a group's response to stress at a macro level. A macro example is how some of the existing vulnerabilities of the Asian American community have been compounded during the present health pandemic of COVID-19 in juxtaposition with the social pandemic due to the longstanding history of police brutality against the Black community. As the first case of COVID-19 occurred in China, anti-Asian racism and hate crimes against Asian Americans increased in early 2020. For many Asian Americans, the emotional distress and fear of physical safety, in conjunction with isolation and overall diminished social spaces for support, heightened an existing vulnerability of Asian Americans as people of color. At the same time, movements against the social pandemic ascended on the heels of the murders of George Floyd and Breonna Taylor, Ahmaud Arbery, and many others at the hands of police officers, the voices of the Black community strengthened throughout the country and mobilized many Americans to advocate for change and the racial Black-White binary that historically displaces Asian Americans from the conversation about race in America, was accentuated. Thus, while on the one hand Asian Americans experienced discrimination and violence or threat of violence due to their race as people of color, the Black-White binary at times precluded them from being meaningfully included in the conversation about race in America. As we consider applying the Resiliency Model to the current Asian American experience, the stressful events in our country-X- (social and health pandemics), our vulnerabilities as Asian Americans-V- (displaced racial minorities in a racialized society; job loss; isolation) and our historical typology-T- (silent suffering and history of mobilization), shape the meaning we make of this time we are in-C- (i.e. God is teaching us something; we are learning how interconnected our world is; health pandemics occur every 100 years and we were due) and the resistance resources we possess-B- (faith; family; church; value of endurance) that contribute to our capacity to problem-solve-PSC- and move toward crisis or adaptation. Each of us have our own unique experiences

A micro example of the Resiliency Model is my parents and much of what I have already shared. My parents have demonstrated profound resilience throughout their early years in Korea and in the 52 years of life they built in America. The trauma and loss they lived through during the war, as well as the aftermath of the war, are beyond my imagination. They were vulnerable (V) as immigrants, facing the hardships of downward social and economic mobility and discrimination with minimal social resources (B). But they worked hard and believed that God had a purpose for their lives beyond their own inclinations and dreams for a better life (C). The social resources they had with the few Korean families they knew, and the German church they attended in Winnipeg, served as buffers and resistant resources (B) to help them through many of the hardships they faced. Combining their tools of survival from their early years in Korea, and the few resources they had in the new country, they were able to forge a new life for our family in Canada and in the U.S. When we finally settled in Southern California, my parents laid down roots that went deep. Growing up in a Christian community where predictability and safety were the mainstay of my social existence, I am grateful for God's provision for my parents and my family in this very particular way.

The Church as a Protective Factor

My cultural and family narrative is one of both traumatic loss and resilience, and I continue to be grateful for the ways that Christian community was one of the most important protective factors in my family's life. I grew up in a Korean immigrant that served as a significant social context for my family. It was by no means a perfect church, but it is where my parents felt fully at ease and at home in their identity as Korean immigrants. Monday through Friday my parents moved through majority spaces, navigating language, culture, and relational dynamics that were secondary to their natural sensibilities. But on the weekends, my parents spent much of their time at church where they were with people who looked like them, ate like them, laughed like them, thought like them, and spoke like them. My family experienced what Falicov refers to as "la cultura cura," the culture that cures. According to Falicov, when we are with people who share the culture of the place from which we came, and create a sense of collective belonging, that experience is curative and is like a balm for the soul. Being connected to one's own ethnic community can provide a psychological, social, and oftentimes an economic safety net that serves as one of the most invaluable resistant resources in the face of stress.

The positive benefits of being with people who share values, and a common identity is an important part of identify formation, particularly in the process of ethnic and racial identity formation for minority populations in America. Although individual experiences create variations on the formation process, the general pattern is one where identification with the majority culture, sometimes at the cost of rejecting one's own cultural identity, swings to the opposite end of the spectrum where strong identification with one's own ethnic and racial culture comes with an awareness of their own marginalization and discrimination by the majority culture. Healthy identity resolution (not that the process ever fully ends) is an integrated identity where there is a pride and appreciation for one's own culture, while holding in complexity the value of the majority culture. It is in this space that we are more likely to embody grace and hospitability toward those who are both different from and similar to us. But an important part of the developmental process is to have a place of security and belonging in one's ethnic community. It is in this place that we are able to recognize the meanings and values of our own culture while living in relationship with others who share aspects of our cultural story. Having mentors and role models of success and health, who share our representatives of our cultural identities, is invaluable for the well-being of the community and the individuals growing up in them. These exemplars of resilience provide important examples for the younger generation to know that it is possible to live in this world with their skin, hair, and eyes with pride and to be valued.

While ethnic minority churches can provide a particular benefit to the immigrant community, the Christian church at large has an opportunity to be a resistance resource to the world, one individual and family at a time. As I consider the story I shared at the beginning about my parents' survival of the Korean War, and then reflect on the role the church played in my family's survival in the U.S. as an immigrant family, I must roll the reel back even further to the early years of my parents' marriage. My parents migrated to Winnipeg, Manitoba Canada in the late 1960s where, at the time, there were no Korean churches where they lived. Nevertheless, my parents attended a small German church where they got married and had their children. There were no cultural brokers, and my parents forged a new path for themselves in this strange new world. The congregants of the church cared for them, supported them, and became family to them. My English name, Christine, was given to me by one of the church members who advised my parents to give their children English names and subsequently gave me the name that was to be a declaration of my Christian faith.

Perhaps healing from the trauma my parents endured will not result from psychotherapy sessions or an outpouring of emotions that will relieve them of their emotional burdens. Instead, it is possible that over the years, there has been a slow healing that has occurred in the context of the Christian communities in which they belonged. The German church in Winnipeg and the Korean church in Loma Linda provided security and stability for my family and is where the relationships served as crucibles for change and growth over the past fifty-two years. I also recognize that not all healing occurs solely by the endurance of relationships and time. Asian Americans are more likely to seek mental health support today than twenty years ago, but there are still distances to go in decreasing the stigma of mental illness and increasing the accessibility of psychotherapy.

For many Asian American families, the psychological, sociological, and physiological impact of unaddressed and unresolved trauma, referred to as "invisible wounds," is real.[10] According to the U.S. Department of Health and Human Services Office of Minority Health findings related to Asian Americans, the leading cause of death among Asian Americans between the ages of 15 to 24 was suicide in 2017. During that same year, Asian American female high schoolers were 20% more likely to attempt suicide than their White counterparts.[11] These statistics do not necessarily reflect the effects of "invisible wounds," but indicate that the need to address mental health distress among young Asian Americans is imperative.

---

[10] Richard F. Mollica, "The Trauma Story: A Phenomenological Approach to the Traumatic Life Experiences of Refugee Survivors," *Psychiatry: Interpersonal and Biological Processes* 64, no. 1 (2001): 60-63, https://doi.org/10.1521/psyc.64.1.60.18242.

[11] CDC, "National Center for Injury Prevention and Control," Web Based Injury Statistics Query and Reporting System (WISQARS), 2016. http://www.cdc.gov/injury/wisqars/index.html.

The church has an opportunity to live out its calling, as the body of Christ, by being an agent of grace and restoration among Asian American families. Where resources such as safety, security, and belonging are absent, the church can fill the void and serve as a protective factor for families. Whether the family is dealing with current challenges, historical trauma, or intergenerational conflict, the church can provide a context for healing through relationships, psychoeducation, and counseling ministries that explicitly acknowledge and address mental health concerns. These recommendations are relevant for any church body, regardless of denomination or cultural majority, but I would implore upon Asian American churches to consider the role of the church as a resource for healing with the particular commitment to addressing mental health and relational health concerns to the Asian American community.

References

CDC. National Center for Injury Prevention and Control. Web Based Injury Statistics Query and Reporting System (WISQARS), 2016. http://www.cdc.gov/injury/wisqars/index.html

Choi, K. W. "Postpartum Depression in the Intergenerational Transmission of Child Maltreatment: Longitudinal Evidence from Global Settings" [ProQuest Information & Learning]. In *Dissertation Abstracts International: Section B: The Sciences and Engineering* (Vol. 78, Issue 12–B(E)), 2018.

Danieli Y, Norris F. H., & Engdahl B. "Multigenerational Legacies of Trauma: Modeling the What and How of Transmission." *American Journal of Orthopsychiatry* 86, no. 6, (2016): 639-651, DOI: 10.1037/ort0000145.

Falicov, C. J. "Training to Think Culturally: A Multidimensional Comparative Framework." *Family Process* 34, (1995): 373-388.

Felitti, V. J., Anda, R. F., Nordenberg, D., Williamson, D. F., Spitz, A. M., Edwards, V., Koss, M. P., & Marks, J. S. (2019). "Relationship of Childhood Abuse and Household Dysfunction to Many of the Leading Causes of Death in Adults: The Adverse Childhood Experiences (ACE) Study." *American Journal of Preventive Medicine* 56, no. 6 (2019): 774–786, https://doi-org.fuller.idm.oclc.org/10.1016/j.amepre.2019.04.001

Kellermann, N. P. F. "Psychopathology in Children of Holocaust Survivors: A Review of the Research Literature." *Israel Journal of Psychiatry and Related Sciences* 38, no. 1 (2001): 36–46.

Kim, T. Y., Kim, S. J., Chung, H. G., Choi, J. H., Kim, S. H., & Kang, J. I. "Epigenetic Alterations of the BDNF Gene in Combat-Related Post-Traumatic Stress Disorder." *Acta Psychiatrica Scandinavica* 135, no. 2 (2017): 170–179, https://doi org.fuller.idm.oclc.org/10.1111/acps.12675

Lester, B. M., Conradt, E., & Marsit, C. J. "Epigenetic Basis for the Development of Depression in Children." *Clinical Obstetrics and Gynecology* 56, no. 3 (2013): 556–565, https://doi.org/10.1097/GRF.0b013e318299d2a8

McCubbin, H. I., & Thompson, A. I. (Eds.). *Family Assessment Inventories for Research and Practice.* Madison, WI: The University of Wisconsin-Madison, 1991.

Mollica, R. F. "The Trauma Story: A Phenomenological Approach to the Traumatic Life Experiences of Refugee Survivors." *Psychiatry: Interpersonal and Biological Processes* 64, no. 1 (2001): 60-63, https://doi.org/10.1521/psyc.64.1.60.18242

NIH, National Diabetes Education Program. "Silent Trauma: Diabetes, Health Status, and the Refugee: Southeast Asians in the United States." 2006.
https://www.aapcho.org/wp/wp-content/uploads/2006/06/SilentTrauma.pdf

Waugh, C. E. & Koster, E. H. W. "A Resilience Framework for Promoting Stable Remission from Depression." *Clinical Psychology Review* 41, (2015): 49-60,
http://dx.doi.org.fuller.idm.oclc.org/10.1016/j.cpr.2014.05.004

Weber, M. C., Pavlacic, J. M., Gawlik, E. A., Schulenberg, S. E., & Buchanan, E. M. "Modeling Resilience, Meaning in Life, Posttraumatic Growth, and Disaster Preparedness with Two Samples of Tornado Survivors." *Traumatology* 26, no. 3 (2020): 266-277,
http://dx.doi.org/10.1037/trm0000210

Xiong, I. "Interrupting the Conspiracy of Silence: Historical Trauma and the Experiences of Hmong American Women" [ProQuest Information & Learning]. In *Dissertation Abstracts International: Section B: The Sciences and Engineering* (Vol. 77, Issue 6 B(E)), 2016.

Yoon, W. K. (forthcoming). *Asian Tragedies in the Americas: Chinese, Japanese, and Korean Stories*. Washington, D.C.: Lexington Books.

Eser Kim

Eser Kim is studying Religious Education, focusing on youth agency in the Korean-Canadian church context at Knox College, University of Toronto. Her passion lies in doing ministry with youth.

A Church that Embodies a Caring Image of God and Accompanies the Lives of Families Bereaved by Adolescent Suicide: Deconstructing Patriarchal Image of God and Giving Language to Grief through Lamentation

Eser Kim
Knox College, University of Toronto

Abstract: Socio–cultural statistics on adolescent suicide and theoretical research about suicide in the history of the Presbyterian Church and Korean American culture, reveal that those who are suicide-bereaved struggle to navigate their pain and to find support in the Korean American Church. In response, this research delves into the reason why the lack of support exists in Korean American churches and what is needed to accompany the families who are suffering the loss of their children, specifically from suicide. This research first identifies the patriarchal image of God as one of the reasons for the lack of a compassionate space for their suffering and argues for the deconstruction of that prevalent traditional image. I argue that the Church must first become a community that patterns itself after a holistic view of God–a God who comforts, laments, and heals–which can create space for those among them who are suicide-bereaved. Theological and biblical resources affirm that by embodying the caring image of God, churches can create a compassionate space for the bereaved and lead to provide language that allows them to grieve through lamentation.

Keywords: suicide bereavement, image of God, Korean American church, lamentation, youth

Introduction

In the United States and South Korea, the overall suicide rate

Vol. 5, 31-50 (2021).

has been increasing over time. As of 2017, suicide has become the leading cause of death for Asian Americans aged 15 to 24.[1] Adolescent suicide has emerged as a significant topic of discourse among Asian North Americans, especially since the rate of suicide is disproportionately higher among minorities.[2] Typically, between six to ten people in the immediate circle of the deceased fall into psychological shock and find it difficult to bounce back from the trauma.[3] Despite the growing number of suicide-bereaved families, the academy and the church have paid inadequate attention to bereaved families.[4] The research on psychological impacts on Korean Americans who are suicided-bereaved, and on ways the church as a whole can support the bereaved family members, are limited.[5]

In the United States, from the mid-1980s onwards, scholars began to study the family dynamics of suicide-bereaved families, particularly the psychology. In South Korea, it was not until the middle of the first decade of the 2000s that one or two studies related to suicide-bereaved families appeared.[6] Given that South Korea outranks all other countries of the OECD for suicidal rates among adolescents,[7] and the highest cause of adolescent death for the past nine years has been suicide,[8] the lack of research is alarming. The importance of suicide-bereaved family support began to emerge only in recent years after the suicide prevention law was enacted in 2011.[9] However, the consensus on how to name "suicide-bereaved families" has not yet been reached.[10] Coming to consensus on

---

[1] "Mental and Behavioral Health: Asian Americans," U.S. Department of Health and Human Services, Office of Minority Health, https://minorityhealth.hhs.gov/omh/browse.aspx?lvl=4&lvlid=54#1.

[2] Andres J Pumariega and Neha Sharma, *Suicide Among Diverse Youth* (Cham, Switzerland: Springer International Publishing, 2018), 2.

[3] Korea Herald Economics, "October, the Month of Preventing Suicide: Suicide-Bereaved Family Are On the Edge," last modified October 8, 2017, accessed September 2020 http://news.heraldcorp.com/view.php?ud=20170908000159&md=20170911003215_BL.

[4] Ibid.

[5] Young-a Kim and Jae-Won Byeon, "Trends and Challenges on Research of Korean Studies in Suicide Survivors," *Korean Journal of Psychology: General* 35 (1), (2016): 43-63.

[6] Ibid., 45.

[7] Yonhap News, "Suicide, Still the First Reason of Adolescent Death," last modified April 18, 2017, accessed November 12, 2017, (Original study provided by Organization for Economic Cooperation and Development) http://www.yonhapnews.co.kr/bulletin/2017/04/17/0200000000AKR20170417150700002.HTML.

[8] Soo Yeon Hwang, "Top reason for adolescent death has been suicide for 8years... 27% experience depression," *JoongAng Daily News*, last modified April 27, 2020, accessed January 19, 2021, https://news.joins.com/article/23763872.

[9] Ibid., 45.

[10] Three popular terms for people who lost their significant others by suicide are: suicide survivor, suicide-bereaved, and suicide loss survivor. However, the term suicide survivor can confuse the person who survived a suicide attempt with a survivor of a family member's suicide. Starting around 2016,

even the terminology shows the awkwardness and discomfort that is felt towards this topic.

Although awareness of adolescent suicide and mental health problems are growing, there is a lack of conversations and insufficient support systems to address these issues within local churches. Churches often lack space in their communities for the suicide-bereaved because the subject of suicide is considered taboo in some cultures and religious settings,[11] especially among Korean Americans. This issue could be remedied through an embodiment of the image of God's care and nurturance. This embodiment will give the church the opportunity to accompany the bereaved as they navigate their trauma, helping them name their suffering with faith language. Since the church has been one of the primary refuges for Korean Americans, becoming a church that creates compassionate space and accompanies the suicide-bereaved must be one of the important features that Korean American churches should demonstrate.

This paper points out that for a church to embody the caregiver image of God that creates compassionate space for the bereaved, that accompanies the bereaved in the process of naming their suffering, it is necessary to understand the critical psychological dynamics that the bereaved undergo and what it is like to live as a suicide-bereaved family in the Korean cultural context. While emphasizing the importance of understanding and supporting the grieving process, I will explore how the church views suicide, the reasons for the lack of space for suicide-bereaved families, and the alternative image the church should embody to create space for the bereaved. Next, I will give a vivid image of what that space will look like within a church that embodies a caregiver image of God. Lastly, I will point out how the church can help the bereaved to address their grief in the midst of suffering. To do that will include rediscovering religious language through lamentation that allows the bereaved to name

---

scholars started to use a term "suicide loss survivor," which gives more agency to the bereaved by suicide. This research uses suicide-bereaved, which implies their grief. Some of these scholars are J. A. Knieper, "The Suicide Survivor's Grief and Recovery," *Suicide and Life-Threatening Behavior*, 29 (4), (1999): 353-364; Sveen, C. A., and Walby, F. A, "Suicide Survivors' Mental Health and Grief Reactions: A Systematic Review of Controlled Studies," *Suicide and Life-Threatening Behavior*, 38 (1), (2008): 13-29; Julie Cerel, Jason H. Padgett, Yeates Conwell, and Gerald A. Reed, Jr. "A Call for Research: The Need to Better Understand the Impact of Support Groups for Suicide Survivors," *Suicide and Life-Threatening Behavior*, 39 (3), (2009): 269-281; Patrick W. Corrigan, et al., "Insight into the Stigma of Suicide Loss Survivors," *Archives of Suicide Research* 33 (2016): 1-10.

[11] Mila Park, "A Study of Adolescent Suicide Postvention in Counseling," *Theology and Praxis*, (42) (2014), 365.

their suffering in faith.

Suicide's Psychological Impact on Korean American Families

Suicide is often spoken of as a symptom of a larger mental health problem, but it also needs to be properly conceptualized within the context of family systems. Suicide is not only related to a single individual, but also influences a whole family. An important part of family systems theory is the concept of reciprocal functioning.[12] Reciprocal functioning describes that individuals in a family are not merely bound together by blood, but also a part of a system that affects each other in terms of emotion.[13] Reciprocal functioning reverberates even further, because conflicts in a family system do not conclude in a single-family generation, but are passed on to the next generation.[14] For instance, regarding suicide, a family dynamic can prompt a person to commit suicide and that death produces effects that are felt by the family members. This explains how the suicide of a family member is likely to cause another suicide, causing a ripple reaction in the remaining family, especially for those who identify with the suicide.[15] Also, the possibility of developing mental disorders, such as depression and anxiety, is higher in families affected by a sudden death.[16] Thus, resolving negative family dynamics has the potential to drastically improve mental health in subsequent generations and be a preventative factor for suicide.

Most bereaved families eventually understand death as an inevitable rite of passage and gain psychological resilience as time passes; however, this resilience is shown less in the families of those who are suicide-bereaved.[17] Studies suggest that the family's grieving process and reaction to a death by suicide differ from reactions to a natural death or even a sudden death. Most notable among these complicated factors are blame, anger, guilt, shame, and stigma. At the root of these psychological stressors is the difficulty, or even impossibility, of finding

---

[12] Michael E. Kerr and Murray Bowen, *Family Evaluation* (New York: W. W. Norton & Company, 1988). 7-8, 20.

[13] Ibid., 143.

[14] Ibid., 291.

[15] Myung Soo Kang, "Family Counseling and Therapeutic Interventions for Suicide Survivors," *Yonsei Journal of Counseling and Coaching*, (4), (2015): 11.

[16] Joseph Richman, *Family Therapy for Suicidal People* (New York: Springer Pub Co, 1986), 14.

[17] Jo-Seph Jeon, "Spiritual & Pastoral Support through Psychological Understanding of Suicide Loss Family," *Theology and Praxis* 58, (2018): 306.

meaning in a suicidal death. Studies show that bereaved families struggle to find the meaning and cause of the suicide. Some react to suicide with resentment and misguided blaming.[18] Others become angry because they feel abandoned by the person who committed suicide. Another common reaction is to feel fury, mixed with a deep sense of guilt. This is especially seen in parents who have lost a child to suicide, where they have the sense of guilt that they failed as parents.

In Korean American families, this sense of failure can come from a discrepancy in English and Korean language fluency,[19] a gap of cultural difference, and absence of the parents at home. About two-thirds of Korean American youth revealed their concerns over their parent's limited English proficiency.[20] This language barrier often limits meaningful conversations between parents and children. It also fails to minimize the gap of different cultural standards of each generation. In addition, most first-generation immigrants spend more time establishing their financial security than other parents,[21] which keeps them away from home. These factors that are found in Korean American families contribute to the parents' feeling of guilt. Failure in childcare makes them doubt their ability as parents and results in a significant increase in hopelessness and depression. Parents also tend to blame themselves for not seeing the signs of suicidal behavior that may have occurred because of the language barrier and for failing to prevent the suicide because of not being there for their children. This sense of guilt eventually evolves into shame.

On top of this intrapersonal shame, social guilt is also placed on the bereaved by society's stigmatization. Jacqueline G. Cvinar introduced the concept of stigma as a central issue in families bereaved by suicide due to society's negative perceptions of suicide.[22] Parents are often condemned and stigmatized for not paying enough attention to their child.[23] These

---

[18] Ibid., 38.

[19] Almost all the parents were fluent in Korean but less fluent in English. "For example, while 99–100% of parents were fluent in speaking Korean, only 21% of mothers and 40% of fathers reported speaking English "fairly well" or "well." In contrast, 95% of adolescents reported speaking English at these levels but only 59% of adolescents indicated this level of fluency in speaking Korean." Eunjung Kim, and Seth Wolpin, "The Korean American Family: Adolescents Versus Parents Acculturation to American Culture," *Journal of Cultural Diversity* 15 (3), (2008): 7.

[20] Ibid., 8.

[21] Ibid., 9.

[22] Jacqueline G. Cvinar, "Do Suicide Survivors Suffer Social stigma: A Review of the Literature," *Perspectives in Psychiatric Care*, 41 (1), (2005): 16.

[23] Kenneth P. Mottram, and Larry VandeCreek, "Understanding Suicide and its Bereavement: A Primer for Chaplains," *Chaplaincy Today*, 21 (2), (2005): 8.

parents tend to share cryptically the reason behind their child's death, which shows the shame and stigma people receive from society.

In Korean American culture, where *chemyun*[24] is important, the impact of a child's suicide is more complicated because shame attacks the suicide-bereaved from both interpersonal and intrapersonal sources.[25] Shame is aroused not only when society stigmatizes a family, but also when a person experiences the conflicting emotions of dealing with the suicide. Self-stigma can occur in Korean Christians more than others because of the extreme self-consciousness due to *chemyun*.[26] In Korean culture, which construes the individual's mistake as damage to the whole community, suicide-bereaved families can react with self-inflicted shame because of the knowledge that their reputation is tainted. For instance, the suicide-bereaved self-inflict shame by thinking what other congregation member would think of one's family member's suicide. When a child dies, the family might self-stigmatize themselves thinking people will assume that the parent failed to raise their child in faith and that the child was not a faithful witness of God.[27]

Chemyun also affects the grieving process of Korean Americans. A cultural assumption in the Korean context is that showing grief is an indication of immaturity. A mature person should take loss in stride.[28] In funerals, suicide-bereaved Christian families tend to hide their tears or even seem callous. Many families feel the shame of the social stigma and try to forget the suicide after the funeral service. They try to create a new environment to shake off the social stigma, but the tendency is to become more and more isolated from social support networks, the workplace, and even family relationships.[29] This social status of being isolated and stigmatized makes it more difficult for the bereaved to create bonds with others. Even though the bereaved need support from the outside and from

---

[24] This term can be translated to mean "loss of face." In Asian cultures, the well-being of the community is prioritized over an individual, which is prevalent despite Korean Americans' residence in the West. Thus, an individual's suicide can lead to the family's loss of face. Andres J Pumariega and Neha Sharma, *Suicide Among Diverse Youth*, 9. Chemyun is also connected to morality and the will to be proud in front of others. Thus, chemyun being violated can be interpreted that one's self-esteem is harmed. Young Mi Woo, "Christian Suicide Family in Korean Chemyun Culture Self-Psychological Understanding of Shame and Christian Counseling," *Journal of Counseling and Gospel*, 27 (2), (2019): 179.

[25] Woo, "Christian Suicide," 179.

[26] Jeon, "Spiritual & Pastoral Support," 309.

[27] Ibid., 309.

[28] Woo, "Christian Suicide," 183.

[29] Cvinar, "Do Suicide Survivors," 16.

their families, because of the stigmatization, the bereaved hesitate to ask for help and isolate themselves.[30]

To Korean Americans, church community can be a double-edged sword; on one hand it provides a support network and on the other, it shames one into isolation. Korean American immigrant churches have been one of the primary sources of social, psychological, and spiritual support. Furthermore, Church has been the primary community in which they can feel a sense of belonging, where they can share the "presence and connectedness with other Koreans."[31] As such, Church can be a source of resilience, social support, and psychological comfort. However, it can also create more isolation when it stigmatizes and fails to provide a compassionate space for the suicide bereaved. Since more than two-thirds of Korean immigrants consider church as their primary community,[32] when they are ostracized from their church, not only have they lost their primary support network, but they find it challenging to find other support circles. Not only do people who are in bereavement need sufficient time to mourn and bounce back from the trauma, suicide-bereaved families also need supportive spaces, to have ways to grieve where they do not have to shy away from everyday life. Before delving into creating a compassionate space for the bereaved, we will briefly explore what is causing the isolation and stigmatization of the suicide-bereaved within the church context.

Historical Neglect of the Suicide-Bereaved in Churches

Why has there been a lack of space for the suicide-bereaved in churches? How do culture and theology affect the practices within the church for suicide-bereaved families? Although some churches provide care for suicide-bereaved families, other than a one-on-one sporadic basis of care, not many tools are provided for those who desire to accompany the suicide-bereaved in their grief. There is also a lack of guidance for helping the suicide-bereaved navigate through their trauma.[33] Certain practices

---

[30] Maureen M. Moore, and Stephen J. Freeman, "Counseling Survivors of suicide: Implications for Group Postvention," *Journal for Specialists in Group Work*, 20 (1), (1995): 42.

[31] Hee An Choi, *A Postcolonial Self: Korean Immigrant Theology and Church* (Albany, NY: State University of New York Press, 2015), 99.

[32] Ibid. 98.

[33] Grief practices related to "well-dying" are emerging in some Korean North American churches. However, aside from education about well-dying, there is almost no education about loss. The dominant means of offering care in the church is the funeral service.

derived from theological concepts and certain governing understandings of God, such as the image of a patriarchal and authoritarian God, come into play in the lack tools for suicide-bereaved families.

It is not uncommon to encounter a theology of suicide that says people who commit suicide are condemned to hell. Although the Bible does not specifically prohibit a person from committing suicide, it indirectly discourages suicide by emphasizing life. The biblical emphasis on the respect for life is one basis for dissuading suicide and encouraging the endurance of suffering.[34] The understanding that suicide is outside of God's plan comes from the words of Exodus 20:13, where Moses prohibits killing in the sixth of the Ten Commandments: "You shall not kill." Suicide is a form of killing. Killing oneself is interpreted not only as a denial of God's sovereignty in life, but also as an attack on the sanctity of life.

Based on this and other evidence in the Bible, foundational leaders of the Church have, throughout history, asserted that suicide is a sin, including Saint Augustine,[35] Martin Luther,[36] and in particular John Calvin,[37] who is considered by most Korean American Presbyterian Churches[38] to be the source of their faith. According to Calvin, committing suicide is walking away from God's command, subverting God's providence, and an act of killing a human, which is a product

---

[34] Park, "A Study of Adolescent Suicide Postvention in Counseling," 365.

[35] One of the most prominent church fathers, Saint Augustine, claims suicide violates the sixth commandment, which prohibits murder. He points out that, unlike the ninth commandment, the sixth commandment does not include the words "your neighbors," an absence that can be interpreted to indicate that its command includes one's own life. Saint Augustine, *The City of God*, trans. Marcus Dods, Modern Library Pbk ed. (New York: Modern Library, 2000), 97.

[36] The founder of Lutheranism, Martin Luther, and who influenced Protestantism by being the leading figure of reformation, did believe that suicide is forgivable and that condemning suicide is unjust; however, he also discouraged suicide by saying that it is a sin. Park, 367.

[37] John Calvin, one of the theologians in whom the faith of the South Korean Presbyterian Church is mainly rooted, asserts that humans should live in preparation for death, but they are never allowed to choose when they leave this life. Jeffrey R. Watt, "Calvin on Suicide," *Church History*, 66 (3), (1997): 464.

[38] Many Korean American churches are predominantly based in Protestantism that has adapted evangelical ideas and approaches. They tend to put emphasis on mission activities, separation from public engagement, individual conversion, and strict adherence to particular religious doctrines. One of the core foundational beliefs of evangelicals that appears in Korean American churches is belief in the sinful human nature that needs salvation. For more information, see Young Lee Hertig, "The Korean Immigrant Church and Naked Public Square." In *Realizing the America of Our Hearts: Theological Voices of Asian Americans*, ed. Fumitaka Matsuoka and Eleazar S. Fernandez, 131-146 (St. Louis: Chalice Press, 2004). Rebecca Y. Kim, *God's New Whiz Kids: Korean American Evangelicals on Campus* (New York: New York University Press, 2006). Jonathan Y. Tan, *Introducing Asian American Theology* (Maryknoll, NY: Orbis Books, 2008).

of human hubris.[39] Based on these teachings, medieval churches made strict laws about religious practices around suicide, such as prohibiting commemoration for suicides in Mass and burials with hymns or versicles.[40] Those who attempted suicide were condemned for their sin, kept distant from the church, and banned from the sacrament for two months.[41] Even though regulations have been eased in the present day, this tradition of considering suicide an ultimate sin has made the church unresponsive to suicide.

Some argue that the emphasis of the image of a Father God is merely a societal tradition that has been passed on and offers no justifiable reason for excluding the bereaved. However, the way in which God is imaged in humans contributes to our notions of human value. The patriarchal image contributes to abuses of power by those at the top, while the marginalized, the suicide-bereaved, tend to be overlooked. Rosemary Ruether writes that the capstone of the patriarchal image is seeing God as a "divine male who created the world as a system of rule of men over women, masters over slaves, and ruler over subjects."[42] This image reinforces the patriarchal reading of Christian doctrines of what is sin, who is a sinner, and who receives salvation.

Since suicide has historically and theologically been perceived as disobedience to God, the church viewed suicide as challenging God's authority and subverting God's plan. Within a traditional, patriarchal image of a God who is fearsome, vengeful, and legalistic, challenging God's authority is unacceptable. A negative view of suicide, combined with an authoritarian image of God, has often stigmatized and aroused shame in suicide-bereaved families. This makes it difficult for churches to facilitate discourse about suicide, thus leading to a lack of support for the suicide-bereaved from the church.

A Holistic Understanding of God:
Deconstructing Patriarchal Image of God

Although the perception of suicide needs to change in order

---

[39] Watt, 466.

[40] Alexander Murray, *Suicide in the Middle Ages: Volume 2: The Curse on Self-Murder,* First ed. (Oxford: Oxford University Press, 2011), 183.

[41] Ibid., 185.

[42] Rosemary Radford Ruether, "Sexism and Misogyny in the Christian Tradition: Liberating Alternatives," *Buddhist-Christian Studies* 34, (2014): 88.

to reach out to the suicide-bereaved, the Church must first become a community that patterns itself after a holistic view of God—a God who comforts, laments, and heals—which can create space for the suicide-bereaved in the church. In short, this means that regardless of what we think about suicide theologically, the church needs to be there for the suicide-bereaved. The current atmosphere and culture of the church are causing suicide-bereaved families to fall through the cracks. However, by changing our image of God and embodying that change as a church, we can empower these families to bounce back from their trauma within the faith context.

Do Hoon Kim, a Korean systematic theologian, stresses that a church that acknowledges the traits of a certain image of God will pattern those same traits and convert those ideas into praxis.[43] Utilizing Miroslav Volf's suggestion that the church follow the Trinitarian image of God,[44] Kim asserts that the phrase "image of God" is not only applicable to an individual but also to the church. The term "image of God" already has a collective character that includes humanity.[45] Hence, the church is in the image of God, therefore it should be a community that acts accordingly. Thus, discovering a holistic image of God by going beyond the patriarchal image is important.

Young Lee Hertig shows this need of discovery in the yearning of an emerging Korean American pursuit of God. The desire of going beyond the patriarchal, omnipotent, almighty God is fueling Korean Americans to pursue a nurturing God that "exemplifies the reciprocal relationship."[46] When the church can act in the image of a caregiver God, the church can create space for suicide-bereaved families and accompany them while they navigate through their pain. Although the Bible describes God as an authoritarian figure, numerous passages express God through caregiving characteristics, such as: giving birth, comforting, nurturing, and mourning.[47] This perspective of God has been neglected in the Korean North American traditional theological viewpoint, but the church should initiate a discourse and develop an image that expresses

---

[43] Do Hoon Kim, "Mo-sŏng-chŏk mok-yang kyo-hoe-lon-ŭi (materna ecclesia pastoralis) mo-saek." [A Search for Maternal Pastoral Ecclesiology], *Church and Theology*, 80 (3), (2016): 208.

[44] Miroslav Volf, *After Our Likeness: The Church as the Image of the Trinity* (Grand Rapids, MI: William B. Eerdmans, 1998).

[45] Kim, "Mo-sŏng-chŏk," 208.

[46] Young Lee Hertig, "Why Asian American Evangelical Theologies?" in *Introducing Asian American Theology*, Jonathan Y. Tan (Maryknoll, NY: Orbis Books, 2008), 159.

[47] Kim, "Mo-sŏng-chŏk," 210.

the caring characteristics of God, creating space for the suicide-bereaved and fostering a more holistic understanding of God. Thus, a more holistic understanding of God will allow both the suicide-bereaved and the image of God to flourish.

The maternal traits of God that are throughout this paper, referencing Julian of Norwich's maternal image of God, are introduced to show the caregiving nature of God. However, this presentation is not asserting that God is a female or a mother, just as God is not a male or a father. Images are not intended to strengthen sociological gender stereotypes. The intent of providing a mothering image of God is to reveal how a one-sided traditional interpretation emphasized the fatherhood of God and neglected the other images of God. Even though the Bible uses traditionally patriarchal language, that does not mean we need to continue making gendered distinctions. The Bible was written within a certain cultural context, which means our view of God can and should transcend some of those constraints.

The caring image of God is scattered yet vivid in the Bible. The Prophet Isaiah describes the relationship between Israel and God as a relationship between a mother and a child in need of comfort.[48] Isaiah demonstrates a robust image of God who carries a child in the womb, gives birth, feeds, nurtures, nurses, has compassion on the suffering, and dandles on one's knees. The God who heals is described in Jeremiah and Ezekiel, where God says, "For I will restore health to you, and your wounds I will heal, says the Lord" (Jer. 30:17 NRSV),[49] and "I will bind up the injured, and I will strengthen the weak" (Ezek. 34:16). Matthew 23:37 and Luke 13:34 also depict God as a mother hen that gathers God's children together. L. Juliana M. Claassens, states that God does not only comfort or heal God's people, but God immerses God's self in their sorrow and cries with them.[50] For instance, in Jeremiah, God says, "O that my head were a spring of water, and my eyes a fountain of tears, so that I might weep day and night for the slain of my poor people" (Jer. 9:1). These descriptions show that God is not only powerful, almighty, and hierarchical, but is also a caring, loving, and healing God.

Julian of Norwich uses the mother metaphor to articulate the loving

---

[48] Ibid.

[49] All scriptural citations are from the New Revised Standard version of the Bible, copyright 1989.

[50] L. Juliana M. Claassens, *Mourner, Mother, Midwife: Reimagining God's Delivering Presence in the Old Testament* (Louisville: Westminster John Knox Press, 2012), 19.

and caregiving nature of God by collecting the scattered, traditionally feminine images of God in the Bible.[51] To Julian, "the statement of God's maternity is no simple invocation or comparison, but a repeated insistent reality."[52] In her book, God is a mother who not only gives birth, but also involves herself in the process of a person's growing up. God forgives the wrongdoing of God's child,[53] listens attentively to the problems the child has, restores and heals the child from a wound, and brings the child into endless peace.[54] This shows God's mercifulness, faithfulness, and love towards God's children. However, the child needs to cry out so the mother can hear the need of the child. Then God will take the child in God's arms, give comfort, ask about the core of the problem, and "give it her breast to still its tears."[55] This God does not want the child to run away in shame because of a mistake; instead, God wishes for the child to run to God and ask for help by trusting in God's love.[56] These images that Julian provides model for the church how to relate with the suicide-bereaved. They are in pain and running away from God because of shame and pain. However, this caring, mourning, and merciful God invites them back into the divine presence of comfort and peace.

Moving away from a conventional and patriarchal understanding of God, while embracing a more holistic understanding of God, can create a more compassionate space for the suicide-bereaved. The suicide-bereaved are the ones who need consolation, just as Israel needed the comfort of God in the book of Isaiah. As represented in the Bible, God, the ultimate caregiver, listens, shows compassion, and invites the Israelites and the suicide-bereaved back to the arms of God when they complain, lament, are discontented, and sigh.[57] These are the traits that need to be reintegrated into a holistic image of God so that congregations can better embody the compassionate care that the suicide-bereaved crave.

---

[51] Jennifer P. Heimmel, "God Is Our Mother": *Julian of Norwich and the Medieval Image of Christian Feminine Divinity* (Salzburg: Salzburg Studies in English Literature, Institut für Anglistik und Amerikanistik, 1982), 69.

[52] Ibid., 49.

[53] Julian of Norwich and Barry Windeatt, *Revelations of Divine Love* (Oxford: Oxford University Press, 2015), 91.

[54] Ibid., 104.

[55] Heimmel, "God Is Our Mother," 63.

[56] Ibid.

[57] Claassens, *Mourner, Mother, Midwife*, 44.

Community that Sits on the Mourning Bench

The church that embodies the image of a caregiver God can accompany the bereaved as companions and provide compassionate space in which the bereaved can share their experiences with one another. Unfortunately, churches are often reluctant to participate alongside those who are grieving. Some people are afraid that they might say something wrong and some do not want to go through emotional turbulence with the bereaved. Some people console the bereaved with flowery words such as "they are in better place" or "God only gives us the amount of adversity we can bear." However well-intended, ill-equipped words may be unhelpful or insensitive to the bereaved. Nicholas Wolterstorff, a theologian who lost his son, says that simply recognizing the pain of the bereaved can comfort them. He says "I need to hear from you that you are with me in my desperation. To comfort me, you have to come close. Come sit beside me on my mourning bench."58 Wolterstorff emphasizes the significance of drawing near and sitting next to the bereaved. People assume that the bereaved need the right words or distance during their grief. However, presence is "infinitely more powerful than anything one can do or say."59 Sitting with them on the mourning bench validates their pain and shows them that they are not abandoned, that their pain is being heard, and that someone is participating in their pain.

In the Bible, we find cases where people sit on a mourning bench with the bereaved. When we look at the biblical character of Job, he is facing a severe hardship: he has lost his health, wealth, and family. Job's friends come to console him. In the latter part of Job, the three friends give ineffective advice, of which God does not approve. However, even though the three friends failed to give constructive advice to Job about what he should have done or what he did wrong, these friends sit with Job for seven days before they start to speak. Job 2:13 says, "They sat with him on the ground seven days and seven nights, and no one spoke a word to him, for they saw that his suffering was very great". As revealed in Job, the church needs to understand that being with the bereaved is important. Romans 12:15 also commands us to "rejoice with those who rejoice, weep with those who weep." As a caregiver church, it is time for us to stop

---

58 Nicholas Wolterstorff, *Lament for a Son* (Grand Rapids, MI: Eerdmans, 1987), 34.
59 David G. Benner, *Presence and Encounter: The Sacramental Possibilities of Everyday Life* (Grand Rapids, MI: Brazos Press, 2014), 72.

keeping our distance from the bereaved and instead sit with them on their mourning bench.

Naming Trauma

While accompanying the suicide-bereaved, what would an educational approach look like—one that embodied the image of a holistic, comforting God? What specific tools does the church need to provide to bereaved families? The church can encourage the bereaved to name their suffering in faith by giving them the language to express their resentments, shame, and anger. Pastors and congregations can say that if something is beyond comprehension in the life of faith, then curiosity, anger, and resentment can be directed towards God. Unlike an authoritative God, a caregiving God listens and mourns with the bereaved.

Lamentation[60] gives grief a language and allows people the freedom to be angry at God, especially when the problem of theodicy is awakened. When religious people experience a traumatic event, such as the suicide of a family member, people can blame God for allowing the event to occur. They feel as though God abandoned them. Thinking that God does not care about them may make people feel more traumatized than the traumatic event itself. Through lamentation, the bereaved can find words to voice their fears and pain. Dorothee Sölle states that "the 'phase of expression' in which sufferers find a language for voicing their fears and pain is all important and cannot be skipped."[61] If bereaved families live without naming their problems in faith, these problems will resurface, or the families will be permanently stuck in their grief. Dobbs-Allsopp asserts that expressing deep sorrow or grief before God allows the bereaved to own their grief, helping the sufferer to "acknowledge the fundamental neediness and lack of sole-sufficiency, vulnerability to external forces beyond our control."[62] The practice of lamenting may seem accusatory toward God, creating a disconnection, but the ultimate goal of lament is to

---

[60] Lament can be categorized in two ways. One way of lamenting involves anger toward enemies and asking God to punish them (Psalm 109). The other frame of lamentation is to understand there are reasons for lament, such as illness or tragedy, for which there is no one to blame. There is no clear cause or subject of an individual's or community's sufferings. Thus, it is only possible to express suffering directly towards God (Psalm 88). In this paper, lamentation is focused only on the second definition.

[61] F. W. Dobbs-Allsopp, *Lamentations: Interpretation: A Bible Commentary for Teaching and Preaching* (Louisville: Westminster John Knox Press, 2002), 35.

[62] Ibid., 37.

hope for restoration and healing through God. Although anger may seem like an emotion that would drive God away, Luke A. Powery states that "anger is a mode of relatedness to God."[63]

If this is so, how can churches help the bereaved to lament? One recommendation is to teach the bereaved families how to lament through the Psalms. Lamenting through the Psalms is significant in two ways. First, the Psalms allow us to see our lives as they are without falling into self-deception.[64] Since a tendency of families that are suicide-bereaved is to ignore their pain, the Psalms can help these families avoid belittling their suffering or the seriousness of their desperate moments. The Psalms can help them to navigate through their trauma. Second, reading the words in Psalms reveal that there is nothing that cannot be placed before God, not even painful experiences.[65] Since the psalmist does not wait until God gives an explanation for one's suffering, but becomes proactive and cries out to God, the psalmist's action reveals a sense of trust, showing the bereaved that whatever they feel or say, God will not reject them.[66] The Psalms encourage the suicide-bereaved to give voice to their grief.

Lamenting can start by urgently calling on God, by addressing God as the psalmists do: "Give ear to my words, O LORD; give heed to my sighing. Listen to the sound of my cry" (Ps 5:1-2); "How long, O LORD? Will you forget me forever?" (Ps 13:1); "Give ear to my prayer, O God... Attend to me, and answer me" (Ps 55:1-2a). The psalmists admit from the start that they have a longing and that they need God.[67] This shows that we can lament no matter where we are in our grief. We do not need fancy language to lament. Additionally, we can pour out grievances against the current situation. The Psalms express personal pains to God, such as loneliness, alienation, physical pain, and the need for guidance.[68] For instance, Psalm 102:3-11 contains a powerful cry of anguish from someone completely overcome with pain, suffering, and defeat. Lamenting through Psalms enables bereaved families to vocalize their suffering and

---

[63] Luke A. Powery, "Lament: Homiletical Groans in the Spirit," *The Journal of the Academy of Homiletics*, 34 (1), (2009): 25.

[64] Walter Brueggemann, *The Message of the Psalms* (Minneapolis: Fortress Press, 1985), 52.

[65] Ibid.

[66] David J. Cohen, "Why O Lord? Lament as a Window to the Human Experience of Distress," in *Finding Lost Words: The Church's Right to Lament,* ed. G. Geoffrey Harper and Kit Barker (Eugene, OR: Wipf & Stock, 2017), 69.

[67] Gene T. Fowler, *The Ministry of Lament: Caring for the Bereaved* (St. Louis, MO: Chalice Press, 2010), 48-49.

[68] Ibid.

helps them to see that they are not the only ones who have felt rejected by God. Furthermore, since the Psalms are the Word of God, God is presently grieving along with the bereaved through the words of the Psalms.

Conclusion

Suicide is a crucial issue among Korean Americans. Not only because of the high suicide rate itself, but also the enormous family pain radiating from that act. Despite the significance of the subject, the church does not host enough discourse or education about suicide-bereaved families. Suicide is not solely confined to non-Christians,[69] it is a national, cultural, and social phenomenon; the church needs to respond by providing support. However, discourse about suicide is often considered taboo in the church because it is perceived as an unforgivable sin against God's providence. The church should recognize itself in the image of a caregiving God, which expresses the nurturing and caring aspects of God and creates compassionate space for the suicide-bereaved to mourn. While being a community for the bereaved, the church can assist the suicide-bereaved by providing religious language that helps them navigate through their trauma.

A church that embodies a caregiver image of God can be more inclusive for bereaved families and for others who are suffering. The suicide-bereaved who can resolve their pain in these churches may not fully recover and still need to live with the reality of the traumatic experience. However, it will not only remind them of the pain, but also of an experience of healing. The scar of their trauma will not remain as shame but as a sign of resilience.

---

[69] The suicide of Christians is not publicized, making it difficult to study. However, based on the data that has been collected, the suicide rate of Christians is similar to that of non-Christians. . Kihyun Kim, *Cha-sal-ŭn Choe-in-ka-yo?* [*Is Suicide a Sin?*] (Seoul: Joy Mission, 2010), 33. Chaeyong Chong, "A Protestant Understanding and the Responsibility of the Church towards Suicide," *Theology and Praxis* 16, (2008): 35-61.

Bibliography

Benner, David G. *Presence and Encounter: The Sacramental Possibilities of Everyday Life.* Grand Rapids, MI: Brazos Press, 2014.

Brueggemann, Walter. *The Message of the Psalms.* Minneapolis: Fortress Press, 1985.

Cerel, Julie, Jason H. Padgett, Yeates Conwell, and Gerald A. Reed, Jr. "A Call for Research: The Need to Better Understand the Impact of Support Groups for Suicide Survivors." *Suicide and Life-Threatening Behavior,* 39 (3), 2009: 269-281.

Chong, Chaeyong "A Protestant Understanding and the Responsibility of the Church towards Suicide." *Theology and Praxis* 16, 2008: 35-61.

Choi, Hee An. *A Postcolonial Self: Korean Immigrant Theology and Church.* Albany, NY: State University of New York Press, 2015.

Claassens, L. Juliana M. *Mourner, Mother, Midwife: Reimagining God's Delivering Presence in the Old Testament.* Louisville: Westminster John Knox Press, 2012.

Cohen, David J. "Why O Lord? Lament as a Window to the Human Experience of Distress." In *Finding Lost Words: The Church's Right to Lament.* Edited by G. Geoffrey Harper and Kit Barker. Eugene, OR: Wipf & Stock, 2017.

Corrigan, Patrick W. et al. "Insight into the Stigma of Suicide Loss Survivors," *Archives of Suicide Research* 33, 2016: 1-10.

Cvinar, G. Jecqueline. "Do Suicide Survivors Suffer Social Stigma: A Review of the Literature." *Perspectives in Psychiatric Care,* 41 (1). 2005: 14-21.

Dobbs-Allsopp, F. W. *Lamentations: Interpretation: A Bible Commentary for Teaching and Preaching.* Louisville: Westminster John Knox Press, 2002.

Fowler, Gene T. *The Ministry of Lament: Caring for the Bereaved.* St. Louis, MO: Chalice Press, 2010.

Heimmel, Jennifer P. *"God Is Our Mother": Julian of Norwich and the Medieval Image of Christian Feminine Divinity.* Salzburg: Salzburg Studies in English Literature, Institut für Anglistik und Amerikanistik, 1982.

Hertig, Young Lee. "Why Asian American Evangelical Theologies?" In *Introducing Asian American Theology.* Jonathan Y. Tan. Maryknoll, NY: Orbis Books, 2008.

Hwang, Soo Yeon. "Top Reason for Adolescent Death has been Suicide for 8 Years… 27% Experience Depression." *JoongAng Daily News*. Last modified April 27, 2020, accessed January 19, 2021. https://news.joins.com/article/23763872.

Jeon, Jo-Seph. "Spiritual & Pastoral Support through Psychological Understanding of Suicide Loss Family." *Theology and Praxis* 58, 2018: 297-327.

Julian of Norwich and Barry Windeatt. *Revelations of Divine Love*. Oxford: Oxford University Press, 2015.

Kang, Myung Soo. "Family Counseling and Therapeutic Interventions for Suicide Survivors." *Yonsei Journal of Counseling and Coaching*, (4), 2015: 9-31.

Kerr, Michael E., and Murray Bowen. *Family Evaluation*. First ed. New York: W. W. Norton & Company, 1988.

Kim, Do Hoon. "Mo-sŏng-chŏk mok-yang kyo-hoe-lon-ŭi (materna ecclesia pastoralis) mo-saek." [A Search for Maternal Pastoral Ecclesiology]. *Church and Theology*, 80 (3), 2016: 192-218.

Kim, Eunjung, and Seth Wolpin. "The Korean American Family: Adolescents Versus Parents Acculturation to American Culture." *Journal of Cultural Diversity* 15 (3), (2008): 108-116.

Kim, Kihyun. *Cha-sal-ŭn Choe-in-ka-yo?* [*Is Suicide a Sin?*] Seoul: Joy Mission, 2010.

Kim, Rebecca Y. *God's New Whiz Kids: Korean American Evangelicals on Campus*. New York: New York University Press, 2006.

Kim, Young-A. and Byeon, Jae-Won. "Trends and Challenges on Research of Korean Studies in Suicide Survivors," *Korean Journal of Psychology*: General 35 (1), 2016: 43-63.

Knieper, A. J. "The Suicide Survivor's Grief and Recovery." *Suicide and Life-Threatening Behavior*, 29 (4), 1999: 353-364.

Korea Herald Economics, "October, the Month of Preventing Suicide: Suicide-Bereaved Family are on the Edge," last modified October 8, 2017, accessed September, 2020 http://news.heraldcorp.com/view.php?ud=20170908000159&md=20170911003215_BL

Moore, Maureen M. and Freeman, J. Stephen. "Counseling Survivors of Suicide: Implications for Group Postvention." *Journal for Specialists in Group Work* 20 (1), 1995: 40-47.

Mottram, P. Kenneth, and VandeCreek, Larry. "Understanding Suicide and its Bereavement: A Primer for Chaplains." *Chaplaincy Today*, 21 (2), 2005: 4-11.

Murray, Alexander. *Suicide in the Middle Ages: Volume 2: The Curse on Self-Murder*. First ed. Oxford: Oxford University Press, 2011.

Park, Mila. "A Study of Adolescent Suicide Postvention in Counseling." *Theology and Praxis*, (42), 2014: 357-378.

Powery, A. Luke. "Lament: Homiletical Groans in the Spirit." *The Journal of the Academy of Homiletics*, 34 (1), 2009: 22-34.

Pumariega, Andres J, and Neha Sharma. *Suicide Among Diverse Youth*. Cham, Switzerland: Springer International Publishing, 2018.

Richman, Joseph. *Family Therapy for Suicidal People*. New York: Springer Pub Company, 1986.

Ruether, Rosemary Radford. "Sexism and Misogyny in the Christian Tradition: Liberating Alternatives," *Buddhist-Christian Studies* 34, 2014: 83-94.

Saint Augustine. *The City of God*. Translated by Marcus Dods, Modern Library Paper Book ed. New York: Modern Library, 2000.

Son, Young Ha. "When Will South Korea Clear its Name of 'Suicide Republic'.. Outranking Other OECD Countries Again." *Hankook Daily News*. Last modified September 22, 2020, accessed January 18, 2021
https://www.hankookilbo.com/News/Read/A2020092210030004232.

Sveen, C. A. and Walby, F. A. "Suicide Survivors' Mental Health and Grief Reactions: A Systematic Review of Controlled Studies." *Suicide and Life-Threatening Behavior*, 38(1), 2008: 13-29.

Tatelbaum, Judy. *The Courage to Grieve: The Classic Guide to Creative Living, Recovery, and Growth Through Grief*. First ed. New York: William Morrow Paperbacks, 2008.

U.S. Department of Health and Human Services, Office of Minority Health. "Mental and Behavioral Health: Asian Americans." Accessed September 24, 2020.
https://minorityhealth.hhs.gov/omh/browse.aspx?lvl=4&lvlid=54#1

Volf, Miroslav. *After Our Likeness: The Church as the Image of the Trinity*. Grand Rapids, MI: William B. Eerdmans, 1998.

Watt, Jeffrey R. "Calvin on Suicide." *Church History*, 66 (3), 1997: 463-476.

Wolterstorff, Nicholas. *Lament for a Son*. Grand Rapids, MI: Eerdmans, 1987.

Woo, Young Mi. "Christian Suicide Family in Korean Chemyun Culture Self-Psychological Understanding of Shame and Christian Counseling," *Journal of Counseling and Gospel.* 27 (2). (2019): 171- 200.

Daniel D. Lee

Dr. Daniel D. Lee is the academic dean of the Center for Asian American Theology and Ministry and assistant professor of theology and Asian American ministry at Fuller Theological Seminary. An ordained Presbyterian minister, Daniel has served in a number of ministry contexts, including campus ministry, chaplaincy, immigrant church, pan-Asian ministry, and multi-ethnic churches. Daniel is the author of the book *Double Particularity: Karl Barth, Contextuality, and Asian American Theology*, and various book chapters and articles.

God's Shalom to All of Ourselves: Integrating the Asian American Double Self

Daniel D. Lee

Fuller Theological Seminary

Abstract: In this article, I pose this double life from the perspective of trauma studies instead of biculturalism, particularly focusing on the idea of a fragmentation that arises out of microaggressive traumas as theorized by psychologist Kevin Nadal. This trauma framing of Asian American identity affords us a set of analytical tools for engaging the specific problem of the Asian American double self and the challenge of integration, of exploring what it means to recover, own, and hold together various elements of ourselves in every context. Additionally, concepts from interpersonal neurobiology, especially attachment theory, will provide heuristic capacity to explain an integrative process towards psychological health, particularly through narrative processing in small groups. While this discussion will be primarily psychological in nature, theology grounds this process of identity as wrought by God our Shepherd, who recovers all the lost selves, gathering them from their scattered fragmentation towards union with Christ, bringing divine shalom, all through the power of the Spirit.

Keywords: Asian American, identity, trauma, theology, psychology

In *Meet the Patels*, a documentary film about the love life and family dynamics of Indian American actor Ravi Patel, he explains how he grew up leading a double life.[1] At home, he was Indian Ravi: speaking Gujarati, hanging with Indians, and watching Indian movies. Outside the house, he was American Ravi: speaking English with American friends and watching American movies. As an adult, Ravi begins dating a white

---

[1] *Meet the Patels*, directed by Geeta Patel and Ravi Patel (Four in A Billion Pictures, 2014).

Vol. 5, 53-74 (2021).

woman, but he finds himself unable to bring her home to meet his parents, ultimately breaking up with her. Was the white girlfriend only dating "American Ravi", and not "Indian Ravi" as well? Does "American Ravi" go home to his Indian parents, or is it only "Indian Ravi" that talks to his parents? We might say that Ravi grew up navigating both worlds as a "bicultural" person, and perhaps even felt quite comfortable in those worlds as two different Ravis. However, it is apparent that he was living two parallel lives, presenting different selves to each of these worlds. More importantly, these two selves were not at peace with each other. Ravi's identity is one of fragmentation, lacking integration of the various parts of who he is.

In this article, I pose this double life from the perspective of trauma studies instead of biculturalism, particularly focusing on the idea of a fragmentation that arises out of microaggressive traumas as theorized by psychologist Kevin Nadal. This trauma framing of Asian American identity affords us a set of analytical tools for engaging the specific problem of the Asian American double self and the challenge of integration, of exploring what it means to recover, own, and hold together various elements of ourselves in every context. Additionally, concepts from interpersonal neurobiology, especially attachment theory, will provide heuristic capacity to explain an integrative process towards psychological health, particularly through narrative processing in small groups. While this discussion will be primarily psychological in nature, theology grounds this process of identity as wrought by God our Shepherd, who recovers all the lost selves, gathering them from their scattered fragmentation towards union with Christ, bringing divine shalom, all through the power of the Spirit.

This article is organized as follows: first, I present the complex nuances of Asian American identity, including the limits of authenticity and the utility of various concepts, outlining two psychological approaches: one oriented towards ethnicity and another towards racial formation. Second, I propose a trauma-informed approach with the idea of fragmentation to understanding the inner dynamics of Asian American identity. Finally, I present a framework for facilitated small groups where participants can share their life narratives as a way of healing and processing as they journey towards a more integrated self, including theological reflections.

The Nuances of Asian American Identity

In the previous decades under the influence of multiculturalism, many people, especially people of color, have come to understand their identity in terms of pursuing authenticity. Philosopher Charles Taylor describes this idea of authenticity as "being in touch" with the true self within, that this connection is thought of as necessary "to be true and full human beings" and also needing social recognition and affirmation of this uniqueness.[2] This idea of an "authentic self" functions for Asian Americans by relying on the existence of a core and true essence within a cultural, ethnic, or racial identity that has been partially or wholly lost because of the forces of assimilation to white culture. While this kind of loss is real and a recovery is part of being whole, the language of "authenticity" or "true self" is inherently problematic because it assumes an essential cultural core, especially if ethnic identity is in view.

The problem of essentialism for ethnic heritage is closely tied to the long history of western Orientalism, the ways in which the East is defined by "its strangeness, difference, exotic sensuousness, eccentricity, backwardness" as well as being "static, frozen, and fixed eternally."[3] Since authenticity is based upon this idea of a true self to which one must be faithful, even if the East is framed with appreciation, there is a danger of self-Orientalizing. Kwame Anthony Appiah identifies the danger of the "Medusa Syndrome," of "ossifying" ourselves by the "collective identities" with its narrow "scripts" of what we are to be and how we are to act.[4] The idea of authenticity must be nuanced so that cultural and social identities are understood as "elements" of our individuality, but not the whole of it.

Indeed, Namsoon Kang offers hybridity as the reality of identity, "the search for the ever-changing nature of [the who we are] as hybrid, decentered, multiple selves."[5] Furthermore, given the reality of multiethnic (meaning those of multiple Asian ethnic heritages), as well as multiracial (Asian-white, Asian-Black, Asian-Hispanic, etc.) identity as "affiliation,"

---

[2] Charles Taylor, "Politics of Recognition," in *Multiculturalism: Examining the Politics of Recognition*, ed. Amy Gutmann (Princeton: Princeton University Press, 1992), 28-30.

[3] Namsoon Kang, "Who/What Is Asian?: A Postcolonial Theological reading of Orientalism and Neo-Orientalism" in *Postcolonial Theologies: Divinity and Empire*, ed. Catherine Keller, Michael Nausner, and Mayra Rivera (St. Louis: Chalice, 2004), 102.

[4] Kwame Anthony Appiah, *The Ethics of Identity* (Princeton: Princeton University Press, 2005), 110.

[5] Kang, "Who/What Is Asian?," 117.

what one self-identifies as must be inevitably included in the mix.[6] There is a performative dimension of our everyday reality of identity, of scripts and roles, that intertwine with societal expectations as well as our own self-projections, longings, and survival instincts.[7]

Theologically speaking, the identities of Asian American Christians are found in Christ, as sons and daughters of God reborn by the power of the Spirit. This spiritual identity has been used by some Asian American Christians as a way of denying their earthy identity as inconsequential.[8] However, having our identity in Christ does not mean that our cultural, ethnic, racial, and other identities are irrelevant. Rather than a colorblind generic humanity that unites with Christ, our glorified resurrected bodies retain our worldly particularities as attested to in Revelation 7:9. In order for people of "every nation, tribe, people, and language" to be recognized as such, their earthly identities must be theologically significant. In fact, in the way God reveals the I-Thou reciprocity in the covenantal relationship with God's people, God affirms how God encounters humanity in our particular identities, times, and spaces.[9] Just as the particular and historical identity of God matters as the Yahweh of Abraham, Isaac and Jacob, our particular and historical identity as Asian Americans matter in our encounter with this God. While these particular social and historical identities should not be totalizing, neither should they be erased, leaving us with a reductive and docetic anthology devoid of ethno-racial features; there is no such a thing as an abstract humanity.

Keeping in mind these complexities and affirmations, I turn to key psychological approaches to Asian American identity. While there are many psychological approaches, I present generally two different approaches, one oriented by ethnicity/culture and another framed by racial identity.

The first approach is about navigating the dominant culture as an ethnic minority and is exemplified by the bilinear model of adaptation by

---

[6] David Hollinger, *Postethnic America: Beyond Multiculturalism* (New York: Basic, 1995), 6-7.

[7] See for example, Shirley Anne Tate, "Performativity and 'Raced' Bodies," in *Theories of Race and Ethnicity: Contemporary Debates and Perspectives*, ed. Karim Murji and John Solomos (Cambridge: Cambridge University Press, 2014), 180-97, and Ju Yon Kim, *The Racial Mundane: Asian American Performance and the Embodied Everyday* (New York: NYU Press, 2015).

[8] Rudy V. Busto, "The Gospel According to the Model Minority?: Hazarding an Interpretation of Asian American Evangelical College Students," *Amerasia Journal* 22, no. 1 (1996): 141.

[9] Daniel D. Lee, *Double Particularity: Karl Barth, Contextuality, and Asian American Theology* (Minneapolis: Fortress, 2017), 65-81.

John Berry and others.[10] This model theorizes the combination of a high or low level of acculturation (dominant cultural competence) with a high or low level of enculturation (competence with one's own cultural heritage). The combination of both variables yields four possibilities: separation, assimilation, marginalization, and integration. Integration with high levels of acculturation and enculturation, or "bicultural competence" as LaFromboise et al. have labeled it, means better mental and psychological health for minorities.[11] As a way of categorizing the various identity strategies regarding the dominant culture and heritage culture, this bilinear model is commendable. However, the relationship between acculturation and enculturation could be understood (or misunderstood) as parallel, being adept at navigating two different worlds with two different lives. Their "bicultural competence" can also easily label those ethnic minority individuals code switching back and forth adroitly between dominant and minority cultures, while yet lacking the consciousness of systemic forces that necessitates the need for this biculturalism.

Given the reality of white normativity, implicit bias, and racial toxicity in our society, especially in parts of the country with low Asian American populations or political power, biculturalism can go hand-in-hand with compliance to white dominance and marginalizing of Asian American selves to subcultures, a compartmentalization of "other" selves for purposes for survival and success.[12] Under biculturalism, acculturation can be a fulfillment of the model minority myth or honorary whiteness, while enculturation affirms the forever foreigner trope, with its goal being adjustment to preexisting societal power structures.[13]

The reason why biculturalism is problematic is its presupposition of a multiculturalist society. Along with the problems of "authenticity", given the specter of Orientalism, multiculturalism is based on the idea of ethnic identities and cultural differences, imagining the world as an

---

[10] John W. Berry, "Acculturation as varieties of adaptation" in Acculturation: *Theory, Models, and some New Findings*, ed. Amado M. Padilla (Boulder, CO: Westview Press, 1980).

[11] Teresa LaFromboise, Hardin L. K. Coleman, and Jennifer Gerton, "Psychological impact of biculturalism: Evidence and theory," *Psychological Bulletin* 114, no. 3 (1993): 395-412.

[12] See Michael Morris, "Standard White: Dismantling White Normativity," *California Law Review* 104, no. 4 (2016): 949-78, and Mahzarin R. Banaji and Anthony G. Greenwald, *Blindspot: Hidden Biases of Good People* (New York: Bantam, 2016). Similarly, Feagin proposes the idea of white racial frame. Joe R. Feagin, *The White Racial Frame: Centuries of Racial Framing and Counter-Framing*, Third Edition (New York: Routledge, 2020).

[13] William Ming Liu et al, "Racial Trauma, Microaggressions, and Becoming Racially Innocuous: The Role of Acculturation and White Supremacist Ideology," *American Psychologist* 74, no. 1 (2019): 143-155.

equal playing field for all peoples, never questioning the foundations of our society that privilege some and oppress others. Ignoring the undue burden upon minorities to work towards adapting well to the dominant society, multiculturalism also ignores the long history and present reality of systemic racism baked into all levels of our society. Multiculturalism continues the foundation established by the Chicago school of sociology, with its problematizing of minorities and stress on assimilation.[14] While the language might be softened, the adaption model does not escape the forces of white hegemony as displayed in this earlier assimilation fixation.

Martin Luther King, Jr. in his speech to the American Psychological Association, questioned the very idea of a "well-adjusted life" because there are "some things concerning which we must always be maladjusted" such as racism, religious bigotry, and militarism.[15] The ethnicity or cultural-identity-oriented approach lacks the ability to interrogate the very idea of adaptation. Not all psychological wellbeing and cultural adjustment is good, when forces of injustice abound.

The second approach, oriented towards race, addresses the weakness of the first approach. While there are others, I will present Jean Kim's Asian American racial identity development theory (AARID) as an example.[16] Kim's model, developed from a qualitative narrative study of third-generation Japanese American women, offers Asian American identity development in five stages: (1) ethnic awareness, (2) White identification, which can be passive or active, (3) awakening to social political consciousness, (4) redirection to Asian American consciousness, and (5) incorporation. This last stage is where "Asian Americans… relate to many different groups of people without losing their own racial identity as Asian Americans." Kim clarifies that while the process is "not linear or automatic," these stages are "conceptually sequential" and roughly mirror human developmental stages of childhood, school age, and so on.

While ethnicity is addressed, this model focuses on racial identity

---

[14] LaFromboise's article begins with the explicit reference to Robert E. Park and Everett V. Stonequist of the Chicago school. For white hegemony and the Chicago school of sociology, See Gary Y. Okihiro, *Third World Studies: Theorizing Liberation* (Durham: Duke University Press, 2016), 22-27.

[15] Martin Luther King, Jr., "The Role of the Behavioral Scientist in the Civil Rights Movement," *Journal of Social Issues* 24, no. 1 (January 1968): 1-12.

[16] Jean Kim, "Asian American Racial Identity Development Theory," in *New Perspectives on Racial Identity Development: Integrating Emerging Frameworks*, Second Edition, ed. Charmaine Wijeyesinghe and Bailey W. Jackson (New York: New York University Press, 2011), 138-160, and Derald Wing Sue and David Sue, *Counseling the Culturally Different: Theory and Practice*, 3rd ed. (New York, NY: Wiley, 1999), 121-142.

because Kim believes that the everyday experience of Asian Americans is subject to racial prejudices and stereotypes. The impact of racism at multiple levels is real and formative for the everyday experience of Asian Americans in explicit and implicit ways, but so are cultural forces as well. The saliency and the impact of race or ethnicity upon the everyday experiences of Asian American individuals or communities vary widely.

The idea of integration from the bilinear model of adaptation is important in that integration represents the ability to bring together and resolve internal conflicts. However, the idea of racial identity must be incorporated into any idea of what integration might be. Also, what does the inner psychodynamics of racial prejudices and stereotypes upon Asian American identity look like? Returning to Ravi's double life from the beginning of this article, I offer microaggressive trauma as a way to define the impact of racism on how fragmentation occurs and what the process of healing and integration can look like.

Microaggressive Trauma and the Double Self

Pointing out how the model minority myth obscures the reality of anti-Asian racism, Chou and Feagin highlight "the major racial barriers and hardships, including damaged psychological and mental health, that Asian Americans face as they try to become socially integrated into a racist society."[17] Given erasure of Asian American history and studies within the U.S. education system, Asian Americans are not any wiser than others about the damage that these racial barriers and hardships cause.[18] The invisibility of everyday racism, which mostly are expressed in equivocal ways, makes seeing the problem all the more difficult.

Coined by Chester Pierce, Derald Sue and others researched and defined "microaggressions" as everyday microinsults, microassaults, and microinvalidations that appear relatively benign, but nevertheless have "detrimental impact."[19] For Asian Americans, these microaggressions are

---

[17] Rosalind S. Chou and Joe R. Feagin, *The Myth of Model Minority: Asian Americans Facing Racism* (Boulder, CO: Paradigm, 2010), 22.

[18] Lee observes the "limited and tenuous" impact of Asian American studies upon our education system and mainstream media. Shelley Sang-Hee Lee, *A New History of Asian America* (New York: Routledge, 2014), 2.

[19] Derald Wing Sue et al., Racial Microaggressions in Everyday Life: Implications for Clinical Practice," American Psychologist 62, no. 4 (2007): 279. Sue argues that this subtle and seemingly innocuous form of racism "many times over more problematic, damaging, and injurious to persons of color than overt racist acts." Derald Wing Sue, Overcoming Our Racism: The Journey to Liberation (San

perpetuated along themes such as "aliens in their own land," "ascription of intelligence," "denial of racial reality," "exoticization of Asian American women," pathologizing cultural values/communication styles," and others.[20] Kevin Nadal's concept of "microaggressive trauma" describes how over time these accumulate to manifest trauma-like symptoms.[21] This "microaggressive trauma" is often misdiagnosed because people suffering from it will inevitably recall their latest microaggression, which in and of itself may not be traumatic. Then, their traumatic reactions can sound overwrought, perhaps even a bit obsessive. For many Asian Americans working in predominately white contexts, their work environment becomes toxic because of these microaggressive traumas that can become debilitating. This is, of course, compounded by blatant forms of active and violent racism experienced by Asian Americans, as we have seen increasingly surfacing during the global COVID-19 pandemic.

Although I will be focusing on this racial dimension, a similar kind of low-grade oppression based on cultural values can happen in Asian American spaces as well. For example, in my personal experience as a pastor in a Korean American church, as well as hearing from Korean American seminarians from my teaching experience, I have seen and heard of stress, trauma, and abuse from the ethnic/cultural front. Whether patriarchy, sexism, ageism, classism, legalism, authoritarianism, nepotism, etc., these oppressions are communicated in the guise of cultural values, such as "being Korean" for example. Just like everyday racism, these everyday cultural stressors add up over time, eventually becoming actively traumatic.

On top of these forces, gender-based microaggressions aggravate the situation for Asian American women within both contexts. Meanwhile, Asian American men face racist tropes that denigrate and emasculate them as asexual, socially lesser, and undesirable as mates.

In trauma studies, children who have suffered abuse or trauma for a long period of time can create a double self, where a good, pure, perfect, overachieving self, untainted by abuse balances out the dirty bad self. Judith Herman observes "when it is impossible to avoid the reality of the

---

Francisco: Jossey-Bass, 2003), 48.

[20] Derald Wing Sue et al., "Racial Microaggressions and the Asian American Experience," *Cultural Diversity and Ethnic Minority Psychology* 13, no. 1 (2007): 72-81.

[21] Kevin L. Nadal, *Microaggressions and Traumatic Stress: Theory, Research, and Clinical Treatment* (Washington, DC: American Psychological Association, 2018), 13.

abuse, the child must construct some system of meaning that justifies it."[22] Also, along with creating a perfectionist self that is "a superb performer… an academic achiever, a model of social conformity,"[23] "fragmentation becomes the central principle of personality organization."[24]   In this sense, Asian American identity can be seen as analogous to having a double self in terms of racial and cultural trauma. Our self-hatred and self-blaming, along with overachieving tendencies, fit the pattern. Traumatic fragmentation, and the concept of the double self, explain Asian American self-hatred and self-blaming in regard to racial-ethnic identity. It also explains the overachieving and perfectionistic tendency towards becoming an "honorary white" or "model minority," which are more of make-believe survival strategies, ignoring what we feel cannot be changed about our racist world.

While it is true that Asian heritages, such as Confucianism and communal dynamics of shame, play a role in perfectionistic and self-hatred tendencies, there are good reasons to question their inflated attribution as an expression as Orientalism, ignoring the racial and societal realities. For example, Jennifer Lee and Min Zhou show how the cultural argument for Asian American high academic achievement belied the more complex "historical, legal, institutional, and social psychological processes."[25] The cultural shame explanation also suffers from the same historical amnesia, given the methodological flaws in honor/shame discourse.[26]

Feeling stuck in an undesirable body that is a target of unwanted attention, a perfect overachieving whiter self is presented to the world, while blaming, pushing aside, or leaving behind the problematic Asian self. As a survival or success strategy, one might adopt a bifurcation where the private/communal "Asian" self is operating at home and within ethnic circles, while the public/societal "American" self is presented to the white-

---

[22] Judith Herman, *Trauma and Recovery: The Aftermath of Violence–From Domestic Abuse to Political Terror* (New York: Basic, 1997), 103.

[23] Herman, *Trauma and Recovery*, 105.

[24] Herman, *Trauma and Recovery*, 107.

[25] Jennifer Lee and Min Zhou, *The Asian American Achievement Paradox* (New York: Russell Sage, 2015), 180.

[26] For an anthropological critique of the problematic essentialism in the honor/shame discourse, see Johannes Merz, "The culture problem: How the honor/shame issue got the wrong end of the anthropological stick," *Missiology* 48, issue 2 (2020): 127-141. For how one of the most significant texts in propagating the idea of Asia being a shame culture intersects with Cold War imperialism, see B. Yuki Schwartz, "The Shame Culture of Empire: The Chrysanthemum and the Sword as Handbook for Cold War Imperialism" in *Feminist Praxis Against U.S. Militarism*, edited by W. Anne Joh and Nami Kim (Lanham, MD: Lexington, 2020), 85-103.

normative world outside.[27] The idea of having two selves is not a cause of concern, but the lack of integration between the two selves, as we see in Ravi's life noted above, is.

Trauma studies also gives us the concepts of intrusion and constriction.[28] Intrusion here means that every microaggression carries the accumulated weight of all those prior past incidents. This intrusion disrupts life by constricting it, causing one to avoid places and situations where one might be exposed to the risk of microaggressions. However, since these everyday incidents are ubiquitous, physical constriction to safe spaces is difficult, although many Asian Americans might avoid certain spaces that they consciously or unconsciously know will not be safe for them. More commonly, this constriction occurs in terms of creating a constricted self for the public—a redacted or truncated self that is more presentable and less visible.

This self-editing, where "unpresentable" Asian parts are repressed when in unsafe contexts, might be positively considered as code-switching or biculturality. In reality, so-called bicultural competence within this framework is a pathological acquiescing of the two selves given the racist forces, both located separately within their respective worlds. For many Asian Americans, this skill of self-editing becomes required for everyday life, unconscious and almost second nature. Furthermore, after years of such practice, the deformed or truncated self have become one's own self-understanding, leading to dissociation from one's body or a fragmentation of the self into pieces. Moreover, even as almost second nature, this constant self-redaction as a "continually active process" can be taxing, draining well-being and creativity.[29]

Along with the psychological costs upon individuals, there are broader impacts of this double life. Even if they are biculturally competent, the inclusion of these Asian Americans in the societal and institutional power structures would not contribute towards diversity and racial justice, but rather aggravate them. They themselves are navigating the systems

---

[27] In their study of Korean American church participation, Hurh and Kim use the categories of private/communal *Gemeinschaft* and public/societal *Gesellschaft* to analyze societal racial pressures and communal ethnic church affiliation. Won Moo Hurh and Kwang Chung Kim, "The Religious Participation of Korean Immigrants in the United States," *Journal for the Scientific Study of Religion* 29, no. 1 (1990): 19-34.

[28] Herman, *Trauma and Recovery*, 37, 42.

[29] Sigmund Freud understood repression as an unconscious and yet still active process. See Stephen Frosh, A Brief *Introduction to Psychoanalytic Theory* (New York: Palgrave Macmillan, 2012), 59.

publicly but at the cost of their integration. The model minority myth is an archetype of a self-redacted Asian American suffering from a double self. This complicity in systemic injustices is a byproduct of self-redaction, where non-whiteness is ghettoized, maintaining white normativity. Because of our racial realities, integration must be politically active, resisting the marginalizing forces of normativity.

Various Asian American theologians have described the struggles of racial trauma as the predicament of "betwixt and between," "marginality," or "liminality."[30] While appreciating these works, the trauma-informed perspective offers an interdisciplinary approach engaging psychological concepts and frameworks. Also, this approach provides another level of specificity, adding to how we can look at Asian American identity, nuancing the complex and multifaceted lived realities, and more importantly guides a possible process towards integration and wholeness.

Process of Integration

If Asian American identity itself can be thought of as an expression of trauma, albeit microaggressive trauma accumulating over time, we can draw from trauma recovery resources to ground our identity formation and processing. In a sense, trauma recovery functions like a metaphor for the journey of identity. Rather than recovery, we are seeking an integrated identity healed from fragmentation. Given the long history and embedded nature of white normative racism, Asian Americans will continue to encounter microaggressions and other racist experiences. Thus, the telos of integration is about having the ability to process racial incidents and detox regularly. As well as to affirm and keep together the various aspects of ourselves that are under attack and that we want to distance ourselves from. While recovery is not the best description of what we are seeking, Judith Herman's understanding of a trauma recovery process can be adapted for our purposes regarding integration.

Herman names elements and stages for recovery from trauma,

---

[30] Peter Phan, "Betwixt and Between: Doing Theology with Memory and Imagination," in *Journeys at the Margin: Toward an Autobiographical Theology in American-Asian Perspective*, ed. Peter C. Phan and Jung Young Lee (Collegeville, MN: Liturgical, 1999), 113-134. Jung Young Lee, *Marginality: The Key to Multicultural Theology* (Minneapolis: Augsburg Fortress, 1995). Sang Hyun Lee, *From a Liminal Place: An Asian American Theology* (Minneapolis: Fortress, 2010).

organized around the themes of empowerment and connection. Healing occurs in the context of a relationship with a therapist who can empower and guide survivors both intellectually and relationally, helping them to see the truth of their experience.[31] Within that guidance, there are three stages or components to recovery: 1) establishment of safety, 2) remembrance and mourning, and 3) reconnection to ordinary life. Herman describes these aspects are having an "oscillating and dialogical nature," with progression being like "a spiral" revising the stages again and again but moving towards "a higher level of integration."[32]

During the first stage, the problem must be named accurately, and safety must be established, both bringing control of the body extending to the environment.[33] The second stage of remembrance and mourning is one of storytelling, where the survivors bring coherence to a fragmented and disembodied memory of their trauma. This testimony involves the cognitive, bodily, emotional, and moral dimensions of the self. As trauma is recalled, the corresponding loss must be mourned. Herman characterized this act of mourning as "the most necessary and the most dreaded task" of this stage.[34] The third stage of reconnection involves developing a new self to engage life again. Along with learning skills to deal with fears and dangers, survivors must reconcile with themselves, learn to reconnect with others, and, for some, find a new mission for social action. Survivors of acute trauma will need to process their trauma within a therapeutic relationship first; however, a support group can later be effective for continuing recovery in a supportive communal context. For these groups, active and engaged facilitation is crucial for the sake of safety and a model of what bearing witness to others' stories looks like.[35]

Incorporating various elements of this trauma recovery framework for Asian American identity processing, for the last five years I have developed and gained experience with a program that involves a class on Asian American identity and a small group for sharing personal narrative, which work together in a complementary fashion. There are various details to both the course and the small group experience, but three core themes are central: 1) training for contextual literacy, 2) facilitated and structured small groups, and 3) the goal of coherent narrative for integration. I also

---

[31] Herman, *Trauma and Recovery*, 133-135.
[32] Ibid., 155.
[33] Ibid., 160.
[34] Ibid., 188.
[35] Ibid., 223.

incorporate and engage theological and spiritual elements throughout these themes.

First, it is crucial to present training for contextual literacy with the introduction of mental categories that enable an adequate narration of the nuances of Asian American identity and experience.[36] Formed in a white-normative educational system, Asian Americans lack knowledge about Asian American history and sociopolitical contexts.[37] Even when the mainstream media or culture covers people of color, because of the deep-seated black-white binary paradigm, Asian Americans are absent or erased from view.[38] Because of this widespread lack of education, Asian Americans as a community lack the collective historical memory to deal with racialized experiences.[39] Socialization, with an adequate contextual language for the complexity of the Asian American context, allows for not only an accurate description and interpretation of our experiences, but also the construction and generation of present and future possibilities.

Cognitive linguistics gives us an insight into the role of categories and concept in processing our experience, revealing that we do not have access to pure or raw experience apart from our mental categories.[40] In fact, this is true even of our memories, which are reconstructed with the categories and presuppositions we have at hand.[41] Therefore, even how we tell the story of our lives is determined by the mental categories available to us. Now, the problem of the white normative education and white normative narratives that inculcate Asian Americans is that, while the assimilated or acculturated self is well-supplied, education of the enculturated self is at best elementary or outright Orientalized, leaving a level of contextual literacy that is wholly deficient or even toxic.

The plan for addressing this cognitive lacuna is a hermeneutical framework entitled the Asian American Quadrilateral (AAQ), which

---

[36] This contextual literacy includes but goes beyond the racial literacy that Anderson and Stevenson theorize. Riana Elyse Anderson and Howard C. Stevenson, "RECASTing Racial Stress and Trauma: Theorizing the Healing Potential of Racial Socialization in Families," *American Psychologist* 74, no. 1 (2019): 63-75.

[37] Chou and Feagin, *The Myth of Model Minority*, 193.

[38] Juan F. Perea, "The Black/White Binary Paradigm of Race: The Normal Science of American Racial Thought," *California Law Review* 85, no. 5 (1997): 1213-1258.

[39] Chou and Feagin, *The Myth of Model Minority*, 219.

[40] For importance of mental categories, see George Lakoff, *Women, Fire and Dangerous Things: What Categories Reveal About the Mind* (Chicago: University of Chicago Press, 1987) and Zoltán Kövecses, *Language, Mind, and Culture: A Practical Introduction* (New York: Oxford University Press, 2006), 17-36.

[41] See for example, Charles Fernyhough, *Pieces of Light: How the New Science of Memory Illuminates the Stories We Tell About Our Pasts* (New York: Harper, 2013).

understands the diversity, hybridity, and complexity of the Asian American experience as the intersection of Asian heritage, migration experience, American culture, and racialization.[42] With four main categories to organize subcategories and concepts, the AAQ allows for a wide range of analytical levels from the bird's eye view of historical movements to the minutiae of individual lives. A contextual literacy, based on the AAQ, also allows for the kind of non-essentializing understanding of Asian American identity that is oriented towards awareness and integration, rather than authenticity and true self. Moreover, with its built-in nuances regarding gender, ethnic heritage, migration generation, skin tone, family dynamics, and other personal proclivities, the AAQ functions as an interpersonal hermeneutic to understand, perceive, and locate oneself, as well as all other kinds of Asian Americans and beyond, more accurately.

One of the key issues is to affirm that these aspects of the AAQ all matter profoundly to God, that God sees them and, thus, we are to acknowledge them in our covenantal relationship with God. The Creator God not only sustains the peoples and the cultures, but also redeems our ethnic heritages so that we can express the gospel in and through it. As God's people were constantly moving in salvation history, our God migrates with us, binding up our weary bodies and securing provisions to build new homes. As the God of the oppressed and marginalized, God notices our reductive and distortive representation in the mainstream culture and affirms the rich plentitude of our humanity. Finally, this God recalls our history and empowers us to navigate the predicament of racialization.

I organize my course on Asian American identity and ministry with the AAQ at its core, working with students learning to interpret Asian American lives through its conceptual categories. In a midterm autobiographical essay, Asian American students use the AAQ to understand their life narrative more accurately and the forces that have shaped it. Through the years, what I have found is that often this assignment led to a profound reassessment of not only the student's memories and their overall life narrative, but also their sense of identity. Given that our identity is formed by the stories we tell about ourselves, this result from the shifts in our life narrative is expectable. Some students have found the new revelations of their lives to be disruptive enough to seek psychological

---

[42] Lee, *Double Particularity*, 45-51

help. For them, the contextual literacy unearthed hidden or unnamed traumas that they had justified or sought to expunge from their memory.

Second, learning the contextual concepts work in conjunction with Asian American identity formation groups, highly structured small groups of four to five members actively facilitated by an Asian American faculty member and offered every quarter. There are classmates and a professor you can interact with in the course, but it is primarily a cognitive and intellectual experience, with emotional and relational dimensions largely restricted to the autobiographical essay assignment. This small group, on the other hand, is framed primarily in terms of relationships and this strict commitment to peers and self establishes the safety required for the work of integration.

These groups covenant together to meet around seven or eight times through the quarter on a weekly basis, sharing and bearing witness to each other's personal narratives. The signed covenant document offers full and active participation, careful confidentiality, and safe community formation. With the facilitator leading in modeling vulnerability, safety, mourning, and affirmation, members are invited to invest in the group's formation. Some of these groups are offered on campus in person, with others offered online. In my experience leading these groups, I have found both formats to be effective in our desired outcomes.

Each meeting is an hour long, which is more about limitations in finding a common time than design, comprising of centering prayer, check-in time, personal narrative sharing, and time for response. The centering prayer focuses on being present in our bodies, scanning every part of our embodied selves, to offer or bring before God's presence. The goal here is connecting with our bodies, knowing that our Incarnate Savior invites us to embodied discipleship and vocation. The check-in time invites members to share life events and related emotions, affirming their diversity and importance. Following the example of the facilitator, each of the members is assigned one week to take part in a personal narrative sharing time, using the general outline of the AAQ, with a focus on discerning its coherence. More on this idea of a coherent narrative and its importance for integration will be explained below. Finally, critical for protecting the group's safety, the responses of the other members are limited to clarification questions, words of appreciation, or sharing what resonates with or is evoked in them. Hearing another person's narrative is as beneficial as sharing one's own, because of the way that diverse Asian

American experiences are shared by others. The members are not allowed to try to soothe or short circuit a sharer's journey with spiritual platitudes about how "God will make everything well" or "redeem all pain".

The third and last theme is about the specific features of the personal narratives shared and received in the formation group, the life story that holds the identities together. Pivotal to the process of integration is the idea of a coherence in personal narratives, of bringing order and reasoning to our disorganized stories. Fragmentation from microaggressive trauma, in a sense, scatters and abandons socially unacceptable selves. Integration means creating "a sense of coherence among multiple selves across time and across contexts."[43] Narrative coherence means recalling lost memories, naming what is ambivalent, and bring ordered relationship between emotions and facts. In scripture, naming is connected to power and authority: Adam names the animals that is entrusted to his care (Genesis 2:20), while Jesus names the demon before he casts them out (Mark 5:9). The act of naming particular experiences with accurate and truthful concepts, as in the AAQ, provides control and power to recover the self and reimagine new possibilities for the future. Narrative coherence works with the categories at hand, so it is possible to have integration as "an honorary white" assimilating towards white normativity, blind to the deep racist structures. This is why the interpretative insights of the AAQ is essential, as well as its politically progressive orientation.

Understood within the terms of interpersonal neurobiology with its modern take on attachment theory, the goal of personal storytelling is a coherent narrative that reflects bi-hemispheric as well as vertical integration of various brain processes.[44] This is how educator Louis Cozolino expresses the power of personal narratives:

> A story well told contains conflicts and resolutions, gestures and expressions, and thoughts flavored with emotion. The convergence of these diverse functions within the narrative provides a nexus of neural network integration among left and right, top and bottom, and sensory, somatic, motor, affective, and cognitive processes

---

[43] Daniel J. Siegel, *The Developing Mind: How Relationships and the Brain Interact to Shape Who We Are*, 2nd ed. (New York: Guilford, 2012), 355.
[44] Siegel, *The Developing Mind*, 336-377.

in all parts of the brain.[45]

Bi-hemispheric and vertical integration is crucial because microaggressive trauma arises from the Asian American body and resides in that same body.

A theological overview of the whole process can be imagined in a pneumological manner. I have discussed the role of the Holy Spirit as the integrator of our fragmented self elsewhere, but here I outline some basic features of my thinking.[46] In Paul's body metaphor for the faith community, some members are considered worthless while others are overvalued (1 Corinthians 12:12-26). Using this body metaphor for the actual body of Asian Americans, in a sense, we can imagine that some selves are overvalued, and some are disregarded. This is where the Holy Spirit brings unity and peace to the body, the whole self. Using a different metaphor, we might imagine that in the process of integration, the Spirit as the shepherd gathers lost memories and selves. This same Spirit is the one that "searches everything" (1 Cor 2:10) and "guides us to all the truth" (John 16:13; Romans 8:26-27). This idea of searching and guiding us into truth is particularly salient for our topic at hand. The Spirit not only unites all Christians to Christ, but also all parts of ourselves to Christ.

Conclusion

As the most complex racial category with no common phenotype, cultural heritage nor language, the Asian American identity with its "heterogeneity," "hybridity," and "multiplicity" can be a source of unwieldy burden for many Asian Americans, especially because so many of them lack adequate training.[47] Trauma studies offers a different set of vocabulary to not only diagnose the dimension of Asian American identity, but also a path to process. My proposal for the process of integration includes the set of concepts and language from the Asian American Quadrilateral, the safety and structure of the formation groups, and the

---

[45] Louis Cozolino, *The Social Neuroscience of Education: Optimizing Attachment and Learning in the Classroom* (New York: W.W. Norton & Co., 2013), 21.

[46] The core arguments presented here are included in my chapter "Spirit of Integration and Solidarity: Asian American Pneumatologies" in *T&T Clark Handbook of Pneumatology*, ed. Daniel Castelo and Kenneth M. Loyer (New York: T&T Clark, 2020), 291-300.

[47] Lisa Lowe, "Heterogeneity, Hybridity, Multiplicity: Marking Asian American Differences," *Diaspora* 1, no. 1 (Spring 1991): 24-44.

coherent narrative that brings all the fragmented selves together. This strategy offers key elements for making sense of Asian American identity and bringing together the public and private selves, while also connecting them to the life of faith in Christ through the integrating work of the Holy Spirit. I offer details on how this is carried out at Fuller to stimulate local experiments towards bringing God's shalom to all aspects of Asian American identity.

References

Alexander, Jeffrey C., Ron Eyerman, Bernard Giesen, Neil J. Smelser, Piotr Sztompka. *Cultural Trauma and Collective Identity*. Berkeley, CA: University of California Press, 2004.

Anderson, Riana Elyse, and Howard C. Stevenson. "RECASTing Racial Stress and Trauma: Theorizing the Healing Potential of Racial Socialization in Families." *American Psychologist* 74, no. 1 (2019): 63-75.

Appiah, Kwame Anthony. *The Ethics of Identity*. Princeton: Princeton University Press, 2005.

Banaji, Mahzarin R. and Anthony G. Greenwald. *Blindspot: Hidden Biases of Good People*. New York: Bantam, 2016.

Berry, John W. "Acculturation as Varieties of Adaptation." In *Acculturation: Theory, Models, and some New Findings*, edited by Amado M. Padilla, 9-25. Boulder, CO: Westview Press, 1980.

Busto, Rudy V. "The Gospel According to the Model Minority?: Hazarding an Interpretation of Asian American Evangelical College Students." *Amerasia Journal* 22, no.1 (1996): 133-147.

Chou, Rosalind S., and Joe R. Feagin. *The Myth of Model Minority: Asian Americans Facing Racism*. Boulder, CO: Paradigm, 2010.

Cozolino, Louis. *The Social Neuroscience of Education: Optimizing Attachment and Learning in the Classroom*. New York: W.W. Norton & Co., 2013.

Fernyhough, Charles. *Pieces of Light: How the New Science of Memory Illuminates the Stories We Tell About Our Pasts*. New York: Harper, 2013.

Frosh, Stephen. *A Brief Introduction to Psychoanalytic Theory*. New York: Palgrave Macmillan, 2012.

Herman, Judith. *Trauma and Recovery: The Aftermath of Violence–from Domestic Abuse to Political Terror*. New York: Basic, 1997.

Hollinger, David. *Postethnic America: Beyond Multiculturalism*. New York: Basic, 1995.

Hurh, Won Moo, and Kwang Chung Kim. "The Religious Participation of Korean Immigrants in the United States." *Journal for the Scientific Study of Religion* 29, no. 1 (1990): 19-34.

Kang, Namsoon. "Who/What Is Asian?: A Postcolonial Theological Reading of Orientalism and Neo-Orientalism." In *Postcolonial Theologies: Divinity and Empire*, edited by Catherine Keller, Michael

Nausner, and Mayra Rivera, 100-117. St. Louis: Chalice, 2004.

Kim, Jean. "Asian American Racial Identity Development Theory." In *New Perspectives on Racial Identity Development: Integrating Emerging Frameworks*, Second Edition, edited by Charmaine Wijeyesinghe and Bailey W. Jackson, 138-160. New York: New York University Press, 2011.

Kim, Ju Yon. *The Racial Mundane: Asian American Performance and the Embodied Everyday*. New York: NYU Press, 2015.

King, Martin Luther Jr. "The Role of the Behavioral Scientist in the Civil Rights Movement." *Journal of Social Issues* 24, no. 1 (January 1968): 1-12.

Kövecses, Zoltán. *Language, Mind, and Culture: A Practical Introduction*. New York: Oxford University Press, 2006.

LaFromboise, Teresa, Hardin L. K. Coleman, and Jennifer Gerton, "Psychological Impact of Biculturalism: Evidence and Theory." *Psychological Bulletin* 114, no. 3 (1993): 395-412.

Lakoff, George. *Women, Fire and Dangerous Things: What Categories Reveal About the Mind*. Chicago: University of Chicago Press, 1987.

Lee, Daniel D. "Spirit of Integration and Solidarity: Asian American Pneumatologies." In *T&T Clark Handbook of Pneumatology*, edited by Daniel Castelo and Kenneth M. Loyer, 291-300. New York: T&T Clark, 2020.

______. *Double Particularity: Karl Barth, Contextuality, and Asian American Theology*. Minneapolis: Fortress, 2017.

Lee, Jennifer, and Min Zhou. *The Asian American Achievement Paradox*. New York: Russell Sage, 2015.

Lee, Jung Young. *Marginality: The Key to Multicultural Theology*. Minneapolis: Augsburg Fortress, 1995.

Lee, Shelley Sang-Hee. *A New History of Asian America*. New York: Routledge, 2014.

Lee, Sang Hyun. *From a Liminal Place: An Asian American Theology*. Minneapolis: Fortress, 2010.

Liu, William, Rossina Liu, Yunkyoung Garrison, Ji Kim, Laurence Chan, Yu Ho, and Chi Yeung. "Racial Trauma, Microaggressions, and Becoming Racially Innocuous: The Role of Acculturation and White Supremacist Ideology." *American Psychologist* 74, no. 1 (2019): 143-155.

Lowe, Lisa. "Heterogeneity, Hybridity, Multiplicity: Marking Asian

American Differences." *Diaspora* 1, no. 1 (Spring 1991): 24-44

Merz, Johannes. "The Culture Problem: How the Honor/Shame Issue Got the Wrong End of the Anthropological Stick." *Missiology* 48, issue 2 (2020): 127-141.

Morris, Michael. "Standard White: Dismantling White Normativity." *California Law Review* 104, no. 4 (2016): 949-78.

Nadal, Kevin L. *Microaggressions and Traumatic Stress: Theory, Research, and Clinical Treatment*. Washington, DC: American Psychological Association, 2018.

Okihiro, Gary Y. *Third World Studies: Theorizing Liberation*. Durham: Duke University Press, 2016.

Patel, Geeta and Ravi Patel, director. *Meet the Patels*. Four in A Billion Pictures, 2014.

Perea, Juan F. "The Black/White Binary Paradigm of Race: The Normal Science of American Racial Thought." *California Law Review* 85, no. 5 (1997): 1213-1258.

Phan, Peter. "Betwixt and Between: Doing Theology with Memory and Imagination." In *Journeys at the Margin: Toward an Autobiographical Theology in American-Asian Perspective*, ed. Peter C. Phan and Jung Young Lee, 113-134. Collegeville, MN: Liturgical, 1999.

Schwartz, B. Yuki. "The Shame Culture of Empire: The Chrysanthemum and the Sword as Handbook for Cold War Imperialism." In *Feminist Praxis Against U.S. Militarism*, ed. W. Anne Joh and Nami Kim, 85-103. Lanham, MD: Lexington, 2020.

Siegel, Daniel J. *The Developing Mind: How Relationships and the Brain Interact to Shape Who We Are*, 2nd ed. New York: Guilford, 2012.

Sue, Derald Wing. *Overcoming Our Racism: The Journey to Liberation*. San Francisco: Jossey-Bass, 2003.

Sue, Derald Wing, and David Sue. *Counseling the Culturally Different: Theory and Practice*, 3rd Ed. New York, NY: Wiley, 1999.

Sue, Derald Wing, Jennifer Bucceri, Annie I. Lin, Kevin L. Nadal, and Gina C. Torino. "Racial Microaggressions and the Asian American Experience." *Cultural Diversity and Ethnic Minority Psychology* 13, no. 1 (2007): 72-81.

Sue, Derald Wing, Christina M. Capodilupo, Gina C. Torino, Jennifer M. Bucceri, Aisha M. B. Holder, Kevin L. Nadal, and Marta Esquilin. "Racial Microaggressions in Everyday Life: Implications for Clinical Practice." *American Psychologist* 62, no. 4 (2007): 271–286.

Tate, Shirley Anne. "Performativity and 'Raced' Bodies." In *Theories of Race and Ethnicity: Contemporary Debates and Perspectives*, edited by Karim Murji and John Solomos, 180-197. Cambridge: Cambridge University Press, 2014.

Taylor, Charles. "Politics of Recognition." In *Multiculturalism: Examining the Politics of Recognition*, edited by Amy Gutmann, 25-74. Princeton: Princeton University Press, 1992.

van der Kolk, Bessel. *The Body Keeps the Score: Brain, Mind, and the Body in the Healing of Trauma*. New York: Penguin, 2014.

Narrative Articles

Rev. Florence Li

Rev. Florence Li is the National Coordinator for Asian Ministries at the American Baptist Home Mission Societies since 2004. Her responsibilities include leadership development, mission engagement, and cultural competency awareness. Rev. Li also serves in the Burma Refugees Commission for the denomination to advocate for the Burma Diaspora Christians who experienced religious persecution and human rights violation. Rev. Li is currently volunteering to serve as the ISAAC Board Chair.

"The Future is Bright as the Promise of God" – Trauma & Resilience of the Burma Diaspora Christians

By Rev. Florence Li

Abstract: Through the common sentiment of refugee experience of those who fled for freedom, came the unspeakable story of the writer's early life and mission work for the Burma diaspora Christians. The legacy of Adoniram Judson of his trials and tragedies, the traumatic journey of the Burma diaspora Christians and the imbalance cultural belief of male and female existence in Asian society, came forth the resilience of an individual, a group, a community and a daunting faith that the future is bright as the promise of God.

Mission has come through a full cycle began with Ann and Adoniram Judson, followed by thousands of ethnic minority Christians who survived religious persecution and landed on American soil, living and witnessing the promise of God to enclose the mission circle. The journey of each, the writer, the Judson, the diaspora Christians are testament of a resilient faith which deem to be aspired in a complex chaotic world.

Keywords: Adoniram Judson, Lion Rock, mission, trauma, resiliency

Prelude

One hot summer night, a young mother held her two daughters by the hand. They walked for miles until they came to a small building next to a bus depot, where lines of double-decker city buses were lining up for passengers. The young woman knocked at the door, calling her husband's name. After some hard knocks with no answer, she banged on the door and a man peeked through a tiny cut on the door. The man did not open the door. Rather, he called the name of the husband and told him to run, and he disappeared from the back door. The young woman was angry and upset, shouted all kind of words while her daughters broke down in tears. She had come hoping to get some money from her husband

Vol. 5, 78-83 (2021).

so she could feed her children who were hungry. With disappointment, she dragged her crying daughters, turned around, and walked back where they had come from.

That young woman was my mother.

When the Communist took over China in the 1950s, my parents fled to Hong Kong as refugees with four of their children. I was born in Hong Kong in the mid-1950 and by 1965, I had five sisters and four brothers. My mother claimed there was no family planning service in Hong Kong in 1960s. My father was happy with one big Chinese family blessed by his ancestors.

Hong Kong was poor and filled with refugees who had escaped from China. My family resettled in a housing project called "H" housing. "H" housings were built in a "H" shape, connected by a common corridor of bathrooms, with two wings of individual families stretched from one end to the other. Each building had seven floors but no elevator. All the food markets, family stores, and elementary schools were on the ground floor.

One dry cold winter, a big fire broke out and burned down the entire housing project. Hundreds of families, included mine, were given a small piece of land on a hillside under the "Lion Rock". Lion Rock was a hill that was given its name because one end of the top looked like a lion's head. The hill had a photogenic view and for the people who lived underneath the hill, deemed to have the lion's roar energy. I grew up under the Lion Rock at the time when the American Baptist missionaries, who had been forced to leave Communist China, had reestablished their mission with the Swatow people in Hong Kong.

Burma (Myanmar today) Diaspora Refugees Pilgrimage

God had planted a seed in me for ministries with the refugees as I recall the story told by my parents who were once refugee themselves. My calling into American Baptist Home Mission Societies (ABHMS) in 2004 affirmed my passion with the Asian communities, particularly the immigrants and Asian Americans who are of Asian descent. As the national coordinator for Asian Ministries, I worked with a diverse group of Asians who are Burmese, Cambodians, Chin, Chinese, Filipino, Indians, Japanese, Kachin, Karen, Koreans, Malaysians, Thai and Vietnamese. There are at least twenty-eight different languages and dialects which made up a huge mosaic, unique ministry in our churches. I believe diversity is a blessing, not a curse.

In the fall of 2006, an influx of Burma refugees, who were primarily ethnic Karen, began to resettle into the U.S. from the refugee camps in Thailand. It was reported by the Burmese pastoral leaders in the U.S., and United Nations High Commissioner for Refugees (UNHCR), that about 150,000 ethnic Karen lived in the camps for almost two decades. Since the mid-1980s, the Burmese military had destroyed many villages and forced the Karen, especially Christians, to flee to Thailand.

The Office of General Secretary initiated the Burma Refugee Task Force and I had the privilege to be the coordinator working with the influx communities, relating them to the American Baptist regions and churches. Not knowing the background of the diaspora communities and their mission relation with the American Baptist, I worked closely with the ethnic leaders, made journeys with them and the Task Force members to the refugee camps and other places.

American Baptist Churches USA Mission History with Burma

On July 13, 1813, Ann Hasseltine and Adoniram Judson from Malden, MA, the first American missionaries landed in the port of Rangoon. They introduced Christianity to the Burmese. Adoniram Judson spent his time working on the English-Burmese and Burmese-English dictionaries, and translation of the Burmese Bible that are still being used today. Ann Judson instituted the first co-educational school and translating portions of the Scripture into Thai.

Both Ann and Adoniram Judson endured numerous hardships where he was jailed and tortured. Ann, lobbying for Judson's release with exhaustion and domestic responsibilities, eventually passed away in 1828, leaving a surviving child whose life was also cut short soon after her death. Judson then married Sarah Hall Boardman in 1834, a widow of George

Boardman, a missionary in Burma. She and Adoniram Judson had a son named Edward Judson. Sarah passed away in poor health in 1844. Judson married a third time in 1846 to Emily Chubbuck and together, they had a daughter named Emily Frances, born in 1847. They also had a son but died three weeks after Judson's death at sea returning to MA in 1850. Emily passed away in 1854 from tuberculosis (*Bless God and Take Courage: The Judson History & Legacy*. Judson Press, 2005).

Ko Tha Byu, the first Karen who were converted into Christianity by Judson in 1828, became an evangelist to the Karen people, who then spread the gospel to the Chin, Kachin, Karenni, Mon, Shan, and others. Along with eighty plus American Baptist missionaries and their families, sent from the Foreign Mission Society (International Ministries today) from 1812-1960s, today there are 1.4 million Christians in Burma, including the Burmese speaking.

Burma - Frozen in Time Since the Mid-1960s

Unfortunately, the military regime took control of the country in mid-1960s and the American Baptist missionaries were no longer allowed in the country. The military also created many arm conflicts with the ethnic minorities, especially with the Chin, Kachin, and Karen civilian armies. Burma is said to have the longest civil war in history.

The Burmese government, on the other hand, imposed the national law of Buddhism and destroyed churches and crosses, turned them into command posts and army supply quarters. Villages and fields were burned, and Christians were tortured or jailed. The invasion of the military resulted in hundreds of thousands of ethnic Chin, Kachin, Karen, and other ethnic groups to flee to neighboring countries, or to the mountains to hide. The Karen fled to the border of Thailand where the Thai government and UNHCR established nine refugee camps housing over 150,000 since the early 1980s. The Chin fled to Malaysia, where over 80,000 lived in crammed housing in the slum areas of Kuala Lumpur. Some hid in the jungles in the earlier stage for fear of arrest, while others went to Mizoram, located Northeast of India. Over 120,000 Kachin have become Internal Displaced People (IDP) along the border of Burma and China. Some made their way to Malaysia and a small number had escaped to the refugee camps in Thailand.

New Land, New Hope - Trauma and Resilience

After decades of refugee life and no apparent change coming to Burma, the U.S. State Department, in cooperation with UNHCR in Asia and the Thai government, began offering the option of resettlement to the Karen, Chin and Kachin refugees. Between 2006 to 2018, nearly 135,000 refugees from Thailand, Malaysia and India were admitted into the U.S. 95,000 of the newcomers who live in 130 cities, both suburban and rural areas in the United States, established their own conventions or associations. Many churches also initiated relationships with local American Baptist regions.

During the pandemic, over 300 people died and 2,000 or more were infected with the coronavirus. Hundreds have lost their jobs, and many struggled from day to day. Yet, in midst of the pain and suffering, they lean on hope and found strength in God.

Tansy Kadoe, a licensed marriage and family therapist of Karen descent, described in her article "Everything Beautiful in its Time: COVID-19, Mental Health, and Resilience in the Karen Baptist Churches in the United States," published by *Christian Citizen* in July 2020, said, "Connecting with God and each other has always been the top coping mechanism for the Karen. Their faith that holds onto the promises of God, regardless of circumstances and consequences, makes it possible for them to be resilient in the face of dangers and death. Karen leaders practice coping skills well, such as acceptance, letting go of the uncontrollable, distress, tolerance, etc." There is no doubt "faith" has been the core guiding light for the Karen people.

In Rosalie Hall Hunt's book, *Bless God and Take Courage: The Judson History and Legacy*, she described the many trials Judson had gone through and at the end, he said, "the future is bright as the promise of God." The diaspora Christians, regardless of all circumstances, adhere to this belief. Mission has come through a "full-circle," first began with Judson and many missionaries after him who served in Burma, and now the diaspora Christians who are here, living and witness as missionaries to us. There are still trials and turmoil in their daily life, and yet, leaning on the promise of God is how the diaspora Christians dealt with their trauma and build resilience as a faithful people of God.

Resiliency Comes in Life Lesson

Growing up in a family of ten siblings, I recall my parents' daily struggle of finding food for the table. Not having enough food and inadequate clothing were traumatic for me and for my siblings. I used to follow my mother to the Buddhist temple, burned incense, offered fruits and poultry, and prayed to the Buddha and ancestors to grant a blessing to the family. The blessing was that we would have enough food and clothing in the household. Thus, I prayed hard and then listened to the fortune-teller interpret the good news. I only wanted to hear the good news and reject all the misfortunes. I did not understand why there were misfortunes in this world and believed those misfortunes had equal meaning with "darkness" and "injustice". Until one day I was told about an eternal God who was above Buddha and my ancestors, and above darkness and injustice. I was illuminated by the word of God, the Bible, and not the fortune-teller.

One darkness and injustice were hearing my mother say, "a girl does not need much education" after I told her I was accepted to a university in the U.S. I prayed hard to God to change my mother's belief. The trauma was in that cultural stigmatization between the value of a female and a male. The trauma played out in our cultural practice and human behavior by the belief that a woman does not hold the same worth as a man, or a woman cannot do the same job as a man. A woman who is called by God would not be the same as a man who is ordained by God. In order to get rid of these traumas associated with darkness and injustice, I must fight against them.

Those who experienced trauma know how to live through trauma and triumph as resilient people. God is in the journey with us during our traumatic moments. The Burma diaspora Christians, who have lived through numerous traumas, have built their capacity to recover from difficulties and toughness. I certainly believe their resilience taught me how to cope with my own trauma by leaning on God.

Anna Kang

Anna Kang has been serving in ministry since 2004 and has planted a church in downtown Los Angeles with her husband Louis. They desire to experience the transforming power of God in their community. They have 3 children, Elijah, Eisley and Ella who keep them on their toes. Anna enjoys laughing and spending quality time with family and friends.

Thawing Frozen Traumas:
A Daughter's Journey Home

By Anna Kang

Abstract: Our journey for our true home girds us to endure the hardships of life. There is a deep place within each of us that remembers who we were created to be and the purposes that we bear in our beings. This is the place where hope resides, where the Spirit dwells and invites us to come.

The thread of resiliency reveals itself throughout this narrative as God is at work at every turn. Even in the darkest places, He's there waiting, nurturing, and carrying the brokenness of the world. It is a snapshot of the Gospel embedded in the story of a young girl who is touched by the traumatic histories of her country and family. We find that the dark night of the soul is long and arduous, and the wrestling will leave us with a limp. Yet, it is in that very place we discover that life isn't about living it, rather it is about discovering the source of life through our living.

As we journey with others in this discovery, may we continue to live life full with the source of life.

Keywords: trauma, resiliency, hope, longing, abandonment

I remember that day, even though most of my other memories are foggy. It felt busy that morning, but I sensed the hesitancy. It was my first week of school. I had started the First Grade a couple of days earlier and was looking forward to going and learning. My halmoni (grandmother) used to walk me to the near-by elementary school on the unevenly paved dirt road and would come get me when the half days were over. That was March 1979 in Seoul, Korea.

I remember the delightful cherry-red peacoat, with the neatly

Vol. 5, 86-102 (2021).

placed gold buttons that made a rectangle in the front. My mom bought it for me as I entered this exciting new journey as a first grader. Based on our daily existence of surviving, I knew it was extravagant because we didn't have much. I wore it on the first day of school, along with an eagerness that expressed itself as a big smile on my face. There is a faded picture somewhere, a frozen image of me with a lei around my neck that also exists in my memory. I remember loving the songs that I learned and the body motions that helped me remember the words. I remember everything being new and hopeful…but that morning felt different.

Two women hushed about, moving quietly and not making eye contact. In my small body I sensed a tension, but because of my anticipation of this new place called school, I didn't question the heaviness I felt because it allowed me to escape the loneliness and chaos at home. When it was time for me to leave the house, no one moved. It wasn't until my older cousin, my mom's oldest sister's son, came by and offered to walk me that I left the house. I later found out that my umma (mom) and halmoni didn't have the heart to walk that last walk with me. I didn't know that would be the last time I would be in my home. I didn't know that time would be the last time I would live with my umma, halmoni, and little sister, Jung Kyung. I didn't know that it would be the end of what I had known all my life.

I don't really remember what I did or learned that day, but I do remember looking out at the big glass windows and seeing the moms and caregivers lined up to pick up their kids. I remember seeing them, or maybe I imagined it since this has replayed in my mind thousands of times. I saw them embracing their beloved son or daughter, tucking them away safely in their arms. I kept poking my head up to make sure that I didn't miss the wrinkly old face that was so familiar to me. One by one, my classmates found where they belonged, until I was there by myself with the teacher. And then it happened. An old lady with a round face, one that was much smoother than my skinny halmoni, came up to me and asked, "Are you Jungmi?" I nodded wide-eyed. She stated matter-of-factly, "You are coming with me." My head spun in confusion as my eyes started brimming with tears and my breathing became shallow as I let out a quiet whimper and moaned, "No." She stood there looking down at me. Out of uncertainty and befuddlement, she threatened me, quietly, but firmly, "I'm going to put you on a bus by yourself if you do not stop crying." I remember my heart stopping as the rest of my body froze and the sobs lodged into my throat. I remember everything stopping at that moment. I think a lot of me froze back then.

I followed her to my new home. She was my dad's second wife's mom. My mom was my dad's third woman; he would go on to have two more wives. I didn't know that my mom and dad decided that I would start living with my dad and his second wife after I started school, and that there would be an "exchange" in the first week of school. I didn't know that my life would be turned upside down at the age of six and that I would live the rest of my life longing for home.

I think she held my hand, but I don't really remember. It felt like I was in a movie where everything else around me was either moving too fast or too slow. Everything was a blur of shapes and colors that whizzed by and slowly dissipated into my consciousness. I frozenly shuffled into my new life.

I was met by a much taller woman than my mom, who looked strong and modern. She wasn't short with soft curves, like I was used to with my umma, and she was older than my very young mom. Her face exuded determination and communicated that she would try her darndest to do right by me. I think I might have even seen a tinge of compassion in her eyes when she looked at me. I felt the struggle of her contempt laced with pity. I was told to call her mom. I was introduced to two older sisters and an older brother whose faces were sour and I felt like an alien standing there. After the awkward introductions, I think my new siblings slowly lost interest in the country bumpkin frozen in place and went about their day.

I stood in that space and stared at the dark wood floor, desperately hoping that I would be rescued or be swallowed up into the deep space beneath me. It was in that place I experienced explicitly what it was like to not belong, to be odd, to be unwanted, to feel contempt, and be disdained simply because I existed. In that place, I longed for home. I longed for the familiar. I longed for the softness of kin. I longed for the accustomed chaos, good or bad, healthy or abusive, I wanted to return to the place I called home.

Many, many years later in seminary, thousands of miles from where I started, I learned about the theology of the already but not yet—where I am already actively taking part in the kingdom of God, yet its fullness of expression would be in the future. For the first time, after I was able to articulate the story of God, my heart's longing made sense to me. Even as I accepted that I have a home in God, where Jesus says there are many rooms in His Father's home, this truth would be ultimately fulfilled in the future. In this journey of going home, I deeply comprehend this universal longing as an accurate part of these sacred steps for humanity as we are wooed by the Spirit and led back home.

My being displaced from my home and my family at an early age was unfortunate and even traumatic. However, it is symbolic for the truth that all of us live in this tension of longing for our true home in our Maker. My pilgrimage allows me to remember in my soul what is true and whose I am, even as I struggle through the dissonance in my reality. As I stood there as a little girl, desiring rescue, there was a Savior who came to rescue me from myself. I still struggle and wonder about my home, physical and spiritual, and I am forever grateful to all who have extended a piece of themselves to let me know that I belong and that I am wanted. It is in this, the already but not yet place, that God invites me to warm those frozen places.

The almost two years that I lived with my first stepmom seemed to be filled with the normalcy of childhood, but it wasn't. I continued going to school, which became a blur without the initial excitement and awe. It became monotonous and scary. There would be interactions with my new brother and sisters that were continued reminders that I was an outsider, the illegitimacy of my father's wandering legacy.

My mom, aunt and grandmother would come to see me occasionally. They would stay and drink soju, a Korean rice wine, with my stepmom. Sometimes my dad would join them. On those evenings, I would hold onto my mom for dear life and beg her to take me back with her. I didn't understand why I was there and why I had to live apart from everything I knew. It simply didn't make sense to me and the adults around me never explained.

I would cry and cry and in desperation, make my mom promise me to take me back with her. She would always relent and assure me that she wouldn't leave me behind. Inevitably, I would fall asleep and wake up to the hollow emptiness of their disappearance. The next time I saw them, I would ask why they left without me. She would tell me that it was because I fell asleep, my poor young mom being traumatized herself. Maybe that's why to this day, it is hard for me to rest. I have this deep sense of anxiety that if I relax, the people I love will disappear. It almost seemed that it was better not to have had hope in the first place.

After having loved the first week of first grade, the rest of the school year felt like meandering through the darkness. I eventually entered the second grade and was placed in the tiger teacher's class. He was known to be the strict teacher. I never talked in class, but I felt an extra sense of anxiety during class because I couldn't ask to be excused to use the restroom. One particular day, I sat in my seat feeling the churning in my stomach, unable to move my mouth or raise my hand. I sat there, feeling drenched in dread like syrup slowly being poured over my head. Small beads of sweat formed on my forehead and I began to feel faint. It seemed like forever, but school was finally over, and I made it outside. Then maybe because I knew I was free, my bowels let go. Both relief and shame washed over me at the same time. This particular mix of emotions would be something that would become familiar to me. I waddled home, with the proof between my legs that I really was disgusting. The foul smell repulsed my stepmom as she scrubbed me and wondered out loud what was wrong with me. But, even drenched in this shame, there was a reassurance in this congruence, that it was the shit that was revolting, not the little girl who was lost in this mess.

My dad wasn't home much, and it was better that way. He used to come home in the middle of the night with the intense desire to nurture his family. Maybe it was because his mom had died when he was Twelve. Maybe it was because he had been a POW in the Korean war. Maybe it was because he was trying to feed the emptiness in himself. Maybe it was because he felt guilty. Maybe it was all the above. He would bring spicy rice cakes and other snacks and would wake his kids up. He would speak loudly, slurring words, and wreaking with the familiar smell of his nightly escapades clothed in alcohol, cigarettes, and a good time! The four of us kids and stepmom would begrudgingly awake, wiping the sleep from our eyes, as well as our resentment, trying to fast forward the agonizing ordeal. Some nights, we would all play our part and appease him so we could go back to sleep. Other nights, when my stepmom was fed up, they would argue. These drunken arguments would usually end with my dad's hands around my stepmom's neck because, according to him, he couldn't stand the screaming. I would be chosen by my brother and sisters as his "favorite" to pull him off and save their mother. These moments would color my world in shades of blue and black. The bluish tint that I saw on my mom's and stepmom's lips as my dad choked out the air in their bodies and the deep black hopelessness I felt all around me.

I can say that my dad was the "most interesting man in the world." I can imagine him holding a Dos Equis, although his choice of beer was Budweiser in the States, while he squatted on the floor playing Hwatu, a Korean card game, with his gambling buddies. He was charismatic and at the same time brutish, enigmatic yet simple, abusive and tender, manipulative and unsuspecting. He has been the constant shadow that has darkened my existence and at the same time protected me from the heat. He was the very reason for most of my early sufferings and the reason I existed at all. Both my mom and dad have told me on separate occasions that my mom attempted to abort me, but that my dad locked her up so she would eventually give birth. I am not sure what that meant exactly, but my dad had a very strong desire to have a family. Even as I write this, it is interesting that I feel so committed to my own family, almost obsessively. I have read that fears and traumas are passed down from generations, even when the threat that had previously existed is no longer present now. I understand that my dad existed in a context, trying to make sense of and did his best to overcome the memories of losing his mom, living under the Japanese colonial rule, the Korean war as a POW, and so much more. My dad passed away in 2008 and we made peace before he was gone, but I am sure that it'll take a lifetime to process the impact of who he was in my life.

Sometime in December 1980 I was picked up by my grandmother and taken to Busan, a city by the beach. I'd never traveled so far. It was a glorious ten-day trip, where I was reunited with my umma. I had no idea that this trip was planned nor why it had been planned. I didn't know how long this would last or what it meant; I just knew that I would be with my home. But when I arrived at my mom's new home, it was different.

It wasn't just the changed physical space, but now attached to her was a baby boy and a new man who came home in the evenings. I am not sure what I thought then, but the confusion of the previous year made me feel vulnerable. At 8 years old, I knew that I couldn't tap into the place that made me feel naked, so I chose anger. I remember feeling so angry! I hated that little boy. I hated that while I was away, this little bald, smiley bundle of cuteness had taken my place. I knew I couldn't compete. He was a boy, and my sin was that I was my father's daughter.

My mom had wanted me to be a boy. She had wanted to give my dad a son and felt that she had failed twice by the time she gave birth to my little sister. Two more sons were given to my dad by his fourth wife and by then, my mom used to tell me that she should have aborted me like she had planned. Even then, and as I write now, I knew that she meant that in love, laced with so much of her own pain. In those words of regret, she had been praying for a different outcome, wishing she could have avoided the heartbreak of separation and so much pain. Looking back, what hurt more wasn't the way my life played out, but rather the continued disconnection and rejection of who I was to my mom. She had to deny my existence as she started her new life. In the system of the 70s and 80s in Korea, and even now, a woman with a past couldn't look forward to a future. Although my mom and dad were not legally married on paper, my sister and I tainted my mom's future. We existed as her nieces or someone she knew but could never be who we truly were. God says that I am fearfully and wonderfully made, that He knit me in my mother's womb (Psalm 139:13-14), yet the untangling of this embedded experience has been a continued struggle.

The ten days I spent in Busan was a preparation and mourning for the next phase of my life. During the day, we would go on excursions to the beach, to the markets, we even got a family picture taken together. My mom bought me new clothes, a beautiful dark blue diary with golden swirls that came with a faux gold lock, and a photo album with our somber family picture in the vinyl sleeve. She wrote reminders of her love for me in the margins of this album, just like I existed in the margins of her life. She asked me not to forget her. In the evenings, my mom's new husband would join us for dinner. I thought that this would be my new life and was elated. But I should have known.

After the ten days, my bag was packed again, and I was ready to be taken back. I couldn't bear it this time. I knew what the separation meant. I knew that I'd be going away from my home. I was taken on a train with my grandmother and I cried out, "Umma! Umma! Umma!" It felt so violent to be taken away, yet again to be ripped apart from the bosom of my home. I wanted to resist with my body and my voice. When the first clunk of the train signaled movement and I heard the screeching sound of the train wheels against the steel tracks, I could feel my heart drop. I wanted to jump out of the prison I felt condemned to and I wanted to crawl out of my skin, to be free. The desire to survive knotted into a tight ball in the pit of my stomach, which would take years to unknot, and gave into a fire of burning rage that I would tap into to propel me forward. I yelled more. I cried harder. I ran toward the back and looked out through the small window. The train started to move slowly at first, but as it picked up speed, I saw my home further and further away, leaving me and me leaving it. Somehow, by having stayed on that train, I felt that I had betrayed myself in this complicit leaving. As my last ten days blurred behind me, I cried the whole 8 or so hours in defeat, back to my stepmom's. It had exhausted my grandmother, I could tell by the way she patted me and then threatened me, her already wrinkled face aging right before my eyes.

In January 1981, after almost two years of living with my dad's second wife, I was on a plane heading to the United States of America. This was the plan all along and why I was able to spend time with my mom before I left the continent, for her to have some closure. I had never been on a plane and the stewardesses were very nice. They were pale and had hair of golden clouds. Their eyes were like glass marbles and they would ask, "coffee, milk, tea?" melodiously with a plastic smile in a language that sounded like babble. This language would eventually help open the portals that would allow me to breathe. I played cards with another girl on the plane who was around my age. I was traveling with my dad and a grandmother I had never met before. I didn't know it then, but she was my dad's first wife's mom. We landed in Portland, Oregon and drove to Beaverton in an orange and white Mustang. I spend the next four-and-a-half years getting accustomed to the American way, experiencing another culture shock that would inform me that I didn't belong, that I was yet again a foreigner.

I met my dad's first wife, Maria, who never had any kids of her own. She had escaped to South Korea from the North with my dad and had credited my dad with saving her life. Maybe that's why, even with all his carousing and womanizing, she invited him to the States. My dad and I lived with her in the low-income housing apartments and she became my third mom. She was small in frame and an oval face with double eyelids. She had longer, wavy hair that she always put up in a loose, neat bun. She was short, but in her presence, you always felt like you needed to stand tall. There were two bedrooms, one for her and one for my dad and me. She was a housekeeper at a local hospital, where she would work for decades. She was quiet and proper, not a yeller like my mom or my other stepmom; I couldn't imagine my dad laying hands on her. She was Catholic.

Maria's house was filled with reminders of God, paintings of the disciples, small statues of Mother Mary, crosses with Jesus still hanging on them, books about heaven and hell, and lots of rosaries. Each wall was adorned with some theological depiction and that made me feel both scared and safe. It was scary. Before I first came to the States, my half-sister told me that if I saw a priest or a nun on TV, that meant that it would be a horror movie like The Omen, which proved to be true. But it was also the first time I recognized a presence bigger than myself and my situation, a spiritual reality that would beckon me. In that truth, I rested safe.

Although I wouldn't call her a hoarder, she kept a lot of stuff. Whenever she would leave for her night shift at the hospital around 3 pm, I would be left by myself at home. I would venture into Maria's room. It was always kept closed and the window was always halfway open. It was always cold, even in the hot summers. I wonder if that's why I always equated Mother Maria as cold, or maybe her room was always cold because she was so unemotional. Her room was full of clothes and trinkets from the past. She loved trinkets. She has many small knickknacks that cluttered her vanity. She had a jewelry box that I would open, filled with costume jewelry, and I'd try it on while making sure to memorize their places so I could place them back in their original spots. Maria's devotion and interpretation of her Catholic faith didn't allow much room for frivolity, so these sparkly pieces seemed disjointed with the serious

Maria. She would never think to miss Mass at the local Korean Catholic church. One Sunday, after a huge car accident in the middle of the night, we both presented ourselves a few hours later at Mass. She was in a neck brace. This rigid piety offered a semblance of structure that I craved and cemented for me a spirituality that lacked flow. I would spend a lot of time in that room connecting with a shadow of a mom, as that was what was available to me.

A lot of times, my dad would be back in Korea with his fourth wife, preparing to bring them to the States to start a new life. He had already brought his second wife and their three kids. They were now living about a mile away from Maria and me. They had come about a month after I came to the States. When they did, Maria asked me who I wanted to live with, them or her? She called me to come into the bathroom and curled my hair, a gift of her time and attention that I will never forget. She used to curl my hair from time to time on special occasions and that always made me feel special. On that evening when she asked me, I really wanted to say that I wanted to be back with my dad's second wife and the kids. Not necessarily because I liked it there, but because it was familiar. When it was time to answer, I heard myself say, "I want to stay here." I think there was something in her eyes that I recognized, a loneliness that I knew so well. I learned that day that I had the power to help people, that if I ignored myself, I could make someone else happy, and then I'd be wanted. This has been very difficult to unlearn and has gotten me into a lot of trouble with some very bad decision making.

I entered the 3rd grade at Merle Davies Elementary school and Mrs. Crawford was my teacher. She had curly red hair that was 80s big, it was poofy. She was older, not like my halmoni old, but old enough that she had wide, thick glasses that made her eyes look as if I were looking into it with a magnifying glass. She was kind. I didn't understand her though. In my class, there was a boy named Chang Ho who was my dad's friend's son. He helped me with simple things like, "Mrs. Crawford, she has to go to the bathroom." He still had "milk cheeks," as people would say, of baby fat with the typical Asian bowl cut. He was nice enough, but I could tell that I was a nuisance. He stayed with me until the 6th grade, his cheeks getting rounder and rounder along with his midsection. Mrs. Bolger in the 4th grade gave us an assignment to make bonnets. I felt so proud that I had sewn a head covering all by myself. It makes me chuckle when I look back and remember a distinctly Asian child wearing a bonnet like Laura Ingalls Wilder. I was neither a pilgrim nor Indian, just a lost little girl without a home and now country.

During this time, I met Ms. Howard. She was absolutely perfect! She had wavy brown hair down to her waist and big, kind brown eyes that looked at me with love. She was my PE teacher, and I would meet her a few times a week in the gym. Her voice was like honey and when she winked at me with her laughing eyes, it was as if we had our own shared language. Unbeknownst to me, she had set up meeting times with me and would pull me out from my regular classroom on a weekly basis to read to me. We would sit right outside of my classroom, by the door and on the floor, and would read to me the new books she had purchased. I don't know why she did this but reading and writing became my absolute favorite subjects. I would inhale the Ramona the Pest collections and later on, reading would become the escape I would need to survive my days. Many years later in my twenties, while in seminary, I found Ms. Howard to let her know how deeply grateful I was to her and for her care during that time of ESL and loneliness. I asked her why she did it and she replied that there was something in my eyes that drew her to me. Knowing what I know about God and how He has chosen to walk with me, I realize that there were many Ms. Howards along the way who have been healing balms to my heart.

Church and Mass were something I never questioned. It was a requirement. Every Sunday I would prepare my heart and mind to meet with God by entering the confession booth. In this holy space, I would recite the sins of the previous week to become worthy enough for the eucharist. Even at 9 years old, I knew that the thin latticed plywood separation between the priest and me was proof that I could never be enough. I would leave the small, self-containing box with the doled-out penance and would know that wasn't enough to clear me because I kept the most grievous sins to myself. As I would recite the Lord's Prayer and Hail Mary's ten times on my knees, I knew that I was an imposter. As I took the wafer into my mouth to let it dissolve on my tongue, the little integrity that I had melted away with it.

But even with my own conflicted experiences, I loved being at church. It was the one place that made me feel like I could be a child. There was Sister Rosemary with glasses who smiled a lot but was strict and taught me about the importance of the altar. It was a place where I could walk in the garden with big statues that recited the story of Jesus, who I held in my arms during a Christmas play. The way Mary held Jesus' limp body told me that mothers loved their children and that gave me a faint hope that maybe, I hadn't been completely rejected. And the way Jesus' face looked back at me, along with the empty grave, gave me reassurance that my present darkness would one day be lifted.

While my dad was in Korea, it would be quiet and empty. Since Maria was working, I would spend my evenings alone doing homework and watching TV. My best friends became the 3 Brady sisters, Captain Kirk, Mr. Rogers, and Bugs Bunny. It was lonely, but it was better this way. When my dad would come back, there was noise, too much noise. He would call his gambling friends to play Hwatu, a Korean card game that made smacking noises when they slapped it down. There was smoking and Budweiser and the frantic cleaning up before Maria came home from work. Then one day, my dad was gone for a long time, maybe like 6 months or so. I never wondered or asked. When he came back, I was told that we were moving to Alaska.

It's a strange feeling when you cannot grieve what you don't know was lost. Leaving Maria was unemotional, and at the same time gut wrenching. And by the way, where was Alaska?! Really? The loneliness I felt while I lived with Maria was like living without a heater in a home during the winter. The years in Alaska felt like I had no home.

I was soon introduced to my third stepmom, my dad's fifth wife who didn't know that I existed until she came to the States and had felt duped into this marriage. My dad's fourth wife, the one that I used to stay with when I would go visit Korea in the summers, had died tragically and he had procured this fifth wife within months to help take care of his two young sons. I found out later that this is why he had stayed in Korea for so long and the reason we had to move as soon as he came back. He was planning his new family of five in Alaska. My first meeting with this woman, who was less than twenty years older than me, was, to say the least, unpleasant. She was shocked that my dad had other children, yet again challenging my right to exist. I was almost fourteen years old and in the throes of teenage angst and she was very unready for this new disappointing life.

My teen years were filled with emotional upheavals. My best friend was Rage and she never left my side. There is a meme on the internet somewhere that says that rage's real name is sadness and that resonates with me. There was so much to grieve. The only way I could survive in those days was to disconnect from that place of sinking and fuel it with something that allowed me to move. My choice of drug was codependency and I used long term relationships to fill the void. I truly believe if I was addicted to a substance, I would have died. It seemed that I recreated drama wherever I went because that was what I was used to. It kept the noise loud enough that I didn't have to befriend the silence that revealed the truth of my reality. It felt hopeless and bleak.

I made choices that were unwise and even harmful. There were those who took advantage of me and my neediness. I used people and they used me. By the time I was nineteen, I had two abortions, was in a dead-end romantic relationship, was physically ill, emotionally exhausted, and suicidal. It was right around this time, I met Christ. It is good news when there is nowhere to go because you feel like you are at your bottom. Unfortunately for me, before I could rise, I had to go even deeper into the hell that was brewing within me. You can call it whatever you like, but I call it the homework that is laid before us that each of us have; it is the prerequisite to experiencing true freedom.

My first year of this new Christendom was fabulous! The highs of exhilarating worship services that were concert-like and the hope-filled possibilities of my future seemed too good to be true. I was at church at least three to four times a week and was eager to do something great for my Savior. It shifted my whole life's direction and it finally felt like I had purpose. God's mercy had led me to experience some supernatural moments of healing and love, and I knew that there truly was a God through Christ Jesus. These moments had made me a believer, that there was a greater reality than the one I was living. My life had changed in an instant through one decision to follow Jesus and I was told that everything would be ok. That was the truth I needed but, looking back now realize that it was a very incomplete lens because even though everything had changed, nothing had changed. To someone who was in deep pain and needed a lot of maturing to do, I didn't understand what a journey of discipleship was. Rather, I was looking for pain relief and I had become addicted to the good feelings that Jesus gave me.

It is no wonder, then, after a year of becoming a Christian while at Bible college, I found myself in deep depression. I questioned why I was still in so much pain and disconnected to the peace He offered, even though everything was supposed to be great because I had Jesus in my life? I prayed fervently, I read my Bible, and I served like a maniac and even then, I still felt alone, afraid, and not enough. In some ways, it was even more difficult experiencing these feelings because I was supposed to be a Christian. It was during this time that I met a woman pastor named Jean Park. I think these are the moments in your life that could be labeled as the perfect storm.

She was young, charismatic and was confident. She had been a missionary to Russia and had brought over female students and was sponsoring them through college. They lived together and she was their "mom". There is nothing in my life that is more appealing to me, as well as painful, than the word mom. Jean Park wanted to take these young people under her wing and mother them. I found myself sucked into this group and became a devoted follower. I was a new believer and I desperately wanted to be taken care of and cut out the pain that had been like a tumor. I ended up quitting school and became Jean Park's shadow.

As I became more deeply involved in this group, I began to depend on Jean Park more and more. I wanted to please her, and she became my god. She started to become more controlling and dictated what we wore, how long we prayed and fasted, what made us holy and how we were going to participate in her ministry. I began to cut off from my other relationships and Jean Park consumed my life. About a year into meeting Jean park, which was about two years of being a Christian, I found myself sitting in a jail cell.

Jean Park wanted to do something great for God as well. Her wounded ego was not satisfied with the smallness of her ministry. In her excitement to gain recognition and acceptance in the male dominated ministry arena, she became zealous to grow her ministry, to support her "disciples". She accepted an invitation from a very concerned young woman to exorcise her sister from the demons that kept her from living her full life. When Kay (not her real name) walked into our lives, I had no idea how much devastation we as a group would cause and how much harm we could inflict on another when we don't work through our own darkness.

Looking back, I do not think that Jean Park set out to harm Kay but, she dehumanized Kay and used her for her own purposes. I haven't talked to Jean Park since 1995, so I am not sure exactly what she was thinking or how she has processed the horrendous events. But as the closest observer of her and her ministry back then, I can say that there were many red flags.

When we picked Kay up from the airport, I remember welcoming her and saying, "hello unni" (older sister), a term Koreans use for those who are older than us out of respect. As soon as those words left my mouth, Jean Park glared at me and sharply chided me, stating that we shouldn't be talking to or addressing demons. After that very first incident, I was not allowed to look at Kay in the eyes or talk to her, because in doing so I would be befriending the demons within her. That set the tone in the home while Kay was with us for the week. We learned to fear Kay and the demons that she "brought" with her. These events made sense because the previous year that we had been living with Jean Park, we had daily prayer meetings that focused a lot on spiritual warfare and casting out various demons in objects that were not holy, as well as people who seemed different than us.

Maybe because my mom and my last stepmom were both astrologists/fortune tellers, and I inherited a spirituality from each of the women that I called Mom, somehow these supernatural events and interpretations made perfect sense. Whether it was because I was avoiding pain, trying to make sense of my life and the complex main characters in it, or trying to be the good daughter that would do anything to not be abandoned, I was groomed for such a leader and for such a time. It's grievous to think that maybe if it hadn't led to such drastic measures as someone dying, that I still might be enslaved to the relationship and spiritual abuse that happened back then. After the exorcism that murdered Kay, the 5 out of the 6 of us ended up in jail. There were many miraculous events that allowed me a second chance at life, and I do not take it for granted.

After being forced to leave the stronghold of Jean Park, I was more lost than ever. But, because surviving is what I was conditioned to do, that is what I did. I worked hard and finished school. I didn't have time for much else. I received a degree in Biblical Studies, and I went to graduate school. When I left for college, where I met Jean Park, I remember fleeing a home that felt way too toxic. By then, I was living with my dad and 2 brothers, all the stepmoms having come and gone. After jail, I had to go back home and the idiom, "from the frying pan into the fire," warned me never to escape from one place of pain for another, like I had done by running from home into the arms of Jean Park and her ministry. So, when it was time for graduate school, I wanted to make sure I left my dad, my home properly. It seemed like I consumed every self-help book I could, I even reached out to a respected Christian author and prayed fervently for healing.

When I got to graduate school, I was once again disappointed in myself because this time I fell into a clinical depression and was suicidal. I couldn't get out of bed and it's only by God's grace that I finished school. It was during this time that I was introduced to Judy, my therapist and now mentor and friend. She walked with me, helping me see more clearly who God said I was and opened her heart to me. I remember Judy asking me in one of our therapy sessions, "How do you see God?" I answered back, "I can't really see him as a father or even mother, but I think I can see him as a therapist!" I know that throughout my life, God had sent many to undergird me, but my work with Judy was a new season of hope and healing. I entered graduate school hoping to eventually teach the Old Testament, but after my theology degree I decided that I wanted to walk with people in their sacred journeys like Judy did with me.

That was almost twenty years ago and so much has happened since then. I have been married now for sixteen years and have three kids. Louis and I have been in ministry from the beginning, and the daily lessons

I have been afforded through this mundane life can only be called a gift, the grace that so many people of faith name and hold onto for their life's journey. The very rock bottom that I hit wasn't something that broke me, it was the very Rock that shattered the false messages that I had clothed on myself. This rebirthing gave me new life. The conditioned responses to the sins of others that shaped who I was, and how I perpetrated sins of my own that impacted others because of who I became, were not easily removed. Partnering with the Spirit of God and allowing a community of safer people to help remold me, has been like childbirth, incredibly painful, yet life-giving.

I still struggle at times when I see old habits and patterns creep up, but I also know that growth and maturity is a process, not a onetime event. I am grateful for my kids and the journey of motherhood that allow me to reparent myself. I am indebted to a community of friends and church family who have been gracious to me, seeing beyond my weaknesses to truly reflect back to me who God says I am, beloved and that I belong. It is in these small steps of kindness and love that God has led me home and will continue to do so, to my eternal home.

↓

Book Reviews

Minor Feelings: An Asian American Reckoning

Cathy Park Hong

New York: One World, 2020. 224 pages. $27.00. Hardcover. ISBN 9781984820365

Review by Joyce del Rosario, Pacific School of Religion

At a time when the dialogue around racial injustice has drawn increased and emerging interest about anti-racism and anti-Blackness, this book offers another approach to conversations that are normally limited to a Black and White binary. Poet Cathy Park Hong's *Minor Feelings: An Asian American Reckoning* is a collection of essays that burrows deep into the Asian American women's experience. Seven chapters bring the reader deep into her psychological and emotional experience while simultaneously outlining some of the external historical events and personal anecdotes that influenced her formation. It is not exactly a chronological biography, but it is a dynamic tracing of Hong's formation.

In the first few pages, Hong hits the tender dilemma of the Asian American experience. When the Immigration Act was lifted in 1965, select professionals from Asia were granted visas to the United States. Hong reminds us that this is how the "model minority" idea came about, a way to say, "See! Anyone can live the American Dream! they'd say about a doctor who came into the country already a doctor" (p. 13). Asian Americans have since become a tool to uphold white supremacy while continuing to

Vol. 5, 105-107 (2021).

belittle Black and Latinx Americans for not being "successful," ignoring the systematic ways in which Black and Latinx communities have been oppressed. This becomes the foundation for what she later describes as "minor feelings".

The second chapter, "Stand Up" is a play on words that poets do so well. Hong discusses Richard Pryor's methods of stand-up comedy acts while describing her own awakening to the need to stand up in her own ways. Minor feelings are "the racialized range of emotions that are negative, dysphoric, and therefore untelegenic, built from the sediments of everyday racial experience and the irritant of having one's perception of reality constantly questioned or dismissed" (p. 55). This is how Hong describes the barely detectable ways in which racial trauma builds up within a person only to also break them down. Minor feelings are the result of becoming honest with oneself and deciding to stand up, the way she offers to do in this book.

This is not a religious book by any means, and yet one can read it with a theological lens because of the way Hong engages racial identity. In some ways it can be read as theological anthropology, or a way of seeing God through the embodied experience of the racialized self. The discomfort of minor feelings leads one to ask, "Who am I and what am I good for?" Minor feelings are reminders to Asian Americans that we do not belong; and yet, there is a hope and a belief that yes, we do, we must. Belonging and identity is often at the heart of theological tasks and Hong brings an honest and raw self to the questions which can often be overlooked with quick Christian quips that cover up our vulnerabilities like fig leaves. Hong offers us the grief of self-reflection on Saturday when church sermons preach the resurrection of Sunday. It is the sentence that is not said enough: "It's okay to not be okay."

In emerging Filipino/a/x American theology, second generation scholars have often cited E.J.R David's *Brown Skins White Minds: Filipino American Post-Colonial Psychology* (2013). Because of the dearth of Filipino American theological literature, scholars have looked to other fields where issues of race and identity have been developed. The ways in which David articulates the internalized oppression of Filipino Americans resonates with Filipino/a/x scholars looking to locate the self in the questions of divine grace, love, and mercy. In the same way, Hong becomes an interlocuter to the intersectional conversation on ethnic identity and gender as it relates to Asian American liberation theology.

That said, Hong writes from a distinctly Korean American woman's perspective. Hong admits to "speaking nearby the Asian American condition, which is so involuted that I can't stretch myself across it" (p. 103). While there are times I am so deeply engrossed in the narrative that I cannot tell her experience from my own, there are other times when I cannot connect at all and read her stories as an exercise of getting to know a stranger. She quotes a friend who says that Koreans are self-hating, but Filipinos, "not so much" (p. 18). E.J.R. David's psychological studies on Filipino Americans would counter Hong's anecdote designed to explore whether or not Asian Americans are all self-hating. It is true, Hong cannot stretch across the wide experiences, histories, and internalized oppressions. It is the minor feelings within the minor feelings that Asian Americans can feel as we look around the room in temptation of comparisons. I find myself both uncomfortable and at the same time relieved that Hong names the nuanced problems within this convoluted category called "Asian American."

In particular, Asian American theology is largely informed by Korean American and Chinese American literature. According to Pew Research, Filipinos are the second largest Asian American group next to Chinese Americans . Harvard Divinity's Religious Literacy project reports that the Philippines is approximately 90% Christian. Yet, I get emails from graduate students across the country asking where they can find more Filipino/a/x American theological resources. Right now, there are very few, although some of us FilAm scholars are working together to develop more literature and research in emerging FilAm theology. Hong's book on "minor feelings" brings up layers of minor feelings within me. I mostly resonate with Hong's Asian American experience and it leaves me longing for something even closer to my Filipina American experience. That is the gift of reading women of color, the intersectionality of whose experiences both resonate and alienate in ways that queer the stereotypes and assumptions of what it means to be Asian American.

Family Sacrifices: The Worldviews and Ethics of Chinese Americans

Russell Jeung, Seanan S. Fong, and Helen Jin Kim

New York: Oxford University Press, 2019. 224 pages. $32.00. Hardcover.

ISBN 9780190875923

Review by Jeff M. Liou

This study of Chinese American familism—"a lived tradition that prioritizes family interdependence and right relationships, through the meaningful rituals of being family"—examines the experiences, values, and practices that emerge from Chinese Confucianism and Chinese Popular Religion.[1] The three co-authors offer a framework for understanding the ultimate concerns of Chinese Americans that have been imprecisely categorized as "nonreligious" in Western paradigms of religion.

Religion in the West is characterized by belief in religious teachings and belonging to religious groups (e.g. denominations). While there is an array of beliefs in Chinese Popular Religion, surveys do not capture the practices (e.g. *fengshui*) that are common to many Chinese Americans. In response to this imprecision, the authors suggest the Chinese concept of

---

[1] p. 6.

Vol. 5, 109-111 (2021).

liyi (禮義) as a schema. *Li* "captures the way life *should* be conducted," including, for example, table manners, while *yi* "refers to the righteousness and duties given one's roles and relationships," for example, between a parent and a child.[2] Taken together, *liyi* "examines (1) what moral practices, or *li*, a given group maintains and values and (2) how they understand and rightly act in their most important relationships."[3] Instead of focusing on the orthodoxy of Chinese American beliefs in contrast to Western Christian doctrines, the authors ask about practices in *situ* and how they honor one's relational responsibilities.

Chapter 2 unfolds many of the features of Chinese Popular Religion that do not easily fit Western religious categories. The chapter rehearses familiar rituals and customs including graveside veneration of ancestors, and the physical arrangement of a home to maximize the flow of *qi*, etc. This "religious repertoire" does not belong to a single belief system and, as the respondents make clear, practitioners can identify as non-religious while partaking of it. Especially interesting is the discussion about religious membership in the history of Chinese thought. Specifically, *conduct* is a significant marker of peoplehood used to distinguish between Chinese kinfolk and otherized "barbarians."

The next two chapters on Transmission and Translation describe the socialization processes affecting successive generations of Chinese Americans. For example, meaningful differences can exist between working class and professional Chinese Americans' regard for the practices associated with Chinese Popular Religion. This leads to differences in the transmission of those practices. Furthermore, the American religious "marketplace" is dominated by Christianity, which acts as a point of comparison for second generation Chinese Americans considering how their values and practices fit in the religious landscape.

The chapters on *yi* and *li* explain Chinese Americans' highest values and common practices. *Yi*, relational righteousness, shows up in Chinese Americans' respect for their ancestors, care for their parents, and sense of responsibility for future generations. One narrative demonstrates the durability of this value despite significant relational disruption in the family system. *Li*, is comprised of the practices that rehearse *yi* values. Family dinners, visits to gravesites in Asia, rotating house parties, Chinese

---

[2] p. 20-21.
[3] p. 22.

language school, and "table traditions" are just some of the examples that many Chinese American readers may recognize as laden with *yi* values.

In the conclusion, the authors gesture toward the contributions that this volume makes to its fields of study. Already, the religiously unaffiliated "nones" (among which Chinese Americans are most likely to be lumped) are known to express spirituality of their own, including belief in God. In his 2014 book, *Latino Pentecostals in America*, Gastón Espinosa observed that the category, "nones" creates a false perception of a move away from religion.[4] The authors of *Family Sacrifices* suggest that applying a *liyi* framework to religiously unaffiliated millennials may add clarity to descriptions of their religiosity and spirituality. Additionally, the authors hint that a shift in the American religious imagination, from belief/belonging to practices, is justified.

As a Taiwanese American pastor and theologian, I read this volume with delight. The important turn from belief/behavior to embodied praxeology/practice theory has been under way for some time. To view culture (including religion) through the unspoken "rules of the game" by which a community operates, and the *habitus* with which an individual organizes her actions has great explanatory power. In fact, to recognize the members of a people group through their practices is not far from recognizing the "people of the covenant" by the faithfulness of their Messiah and their just and faithful participation in the renewal of "all things." I do intend to gesture here toward the New Perspective on Paul. Yet, I do not mean that Chinese American religiosity finds an easier inroad to Christianity through this decidedly Western conversation. Rather, I intend that Chinese American religious habits have something to say to the interpretation of the Pauline corpus.

To characterize a people group by their practices invokes the specter of essentialism. An individual's conduct or intersectional identity may be judged by its alignment with their culture of origin. Many Chinese Americans know the sting of being deemed "not Chinese enough." In my own judgment, turning too hard to practices raises its own problems. Those walking alongside Chinese American Christians, as they navigate both Chinese familism and covenant faithfulness, have a precious resource in this volume.

---

[4] Gastón Espinosa. *Latino Pentecostals in America*. Cambridge, Massachusetts: Harvard University Press, 2014.

Annual ISAAC Journal Subscription

We offer several subscription options

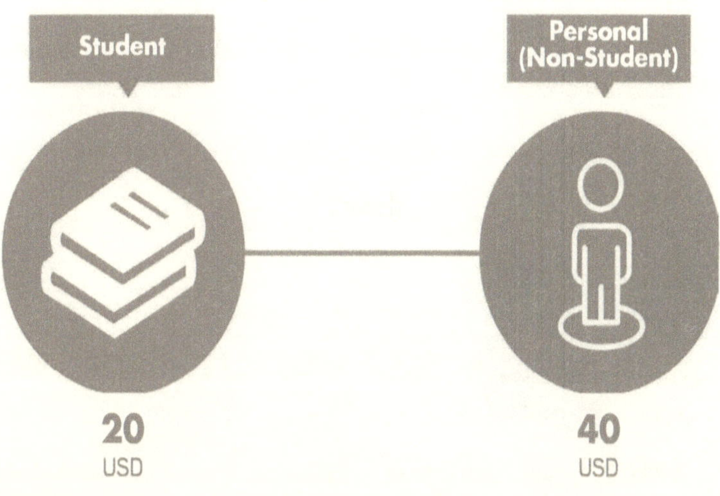

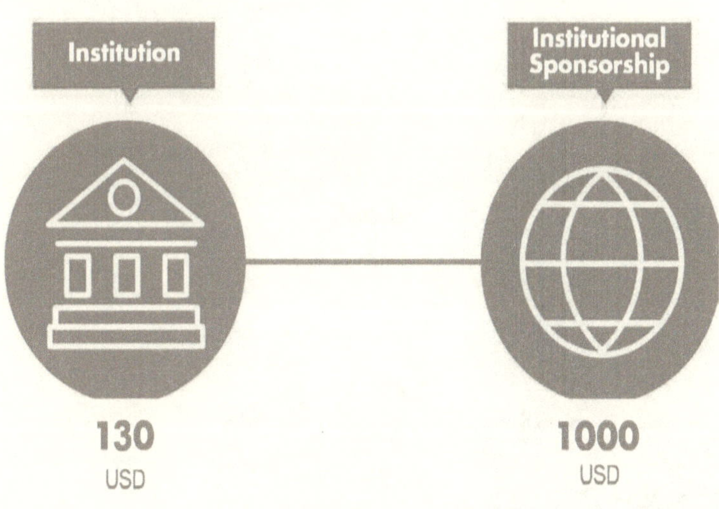